"I have known Jerod Hoffman for more than ten years in his Sr. Leader Peer Advisory team. In WHAT HAPPENS WHEN I DIE you will see principles of 'living proof' testimonies to address the most important question in life. This book gives you a framework to determine where you and those around you are in their spiritual journey. You will learn practical ways to come closer and ultimately answer this question to settle it for eternity. It's been said, you can't really live until you're assured of life forever.

The goal is to challenge you to recognize that we are, in fact, ambassadors for Christ on earth as we enter into a personal relationship with Him and represent him to those around us. We become living proof of His love, grace, and mercy until the day of transition into eternity. This is a must read if the question of eternity has ever rolled into your mind."

Donald W. Hoffert - Servant
Sr. Area Director - Northland CBMC
Christian Business Men's Connection

"WHAT HAPPENS WHEN I DIE? is a great resource for people investigating the answer to this question, as well as leaders, mentors, pastors, churches, and organizations looking to help others

answer this question. In particular, beyond the quality content that is personal and relatable, this book carries moral authority because of Jerod Hoffman's faithfulness to Christ, to the local expression Christ's Body for over thirty years here at Emmanuel, and to complete this book in obedience to God's direction."

Chad Spinler
Emmanuel Christian Center Pastoral Staff
Spring Lake Park, Minnesota

What Happens When I Die?

Is "Being Good" Good Enough?

Jerod Hoffman

Copyright © 2025 Jerod Hoffman All rights reserved.

No part of this publication may be reproduced, stored, or transmitted in any form or by any means, including written, copied, or electronically, without prior written permission from the author or his agents. The only exception is brief quotations in printed reviews. Short excerpts may be used with the publisher's or author's expressed written permission.

All Scripture quotations, unless otherwise noted, are from the New Living Translation of the Bible, Copyright © 1996, 2004, 2015 by Tyndale House Foundation. Used by permission of Tyndale House Publishers, Inc., Carol Stream, Illinois 60188. All rights reserved.

What Happens When I Die?

Is "Being Good" Good Enough?

Cover and Interior Page design by True Potential, Inc.

ISBN: (Paperback): 9781960024886

ISBN (Hardcover): 9781960024923

ISBN: (e-book): 9781960024893

True Potential, Inc.
PO Box 904, Travelers Rest, SC 29690
www.truepotentialmedia.com
Produced and Printed in the United States of America.

Contents

Introduction	7
1: The Most Important Question in Life	11
2: What Does Good Enough Mean?	17
3: Exploring Critical Questions Through Jesus' Words	23
3.1: Is There Only One True God?	27
3.2: How Good Are We Really?	31
3.3: What Does Hell Look Like?	34
3.4: What Does Heaven Look Like?	38
3.5: Who Is Going to Hell and Who Is Going to Heaven?	49
4: The Ultimate Dare	63
5: Decision Time	69
6: Followers -- What's Next?	91
7: Final Thoughts	109
Appendix -- My Story	111

Introduction

It can be so easy in life to focus only on our day-to-day needs, wants, and desires. We make a plan for the day and for the week, and then we work it out. We focus on questions like: what's on our schedule for the week, what are we excited about, what do we need to complete, who should we make plans with, when should we do the grocery shopping, etc. And then the next day we wake up and do this again. And then the next week we reboot the system and do it all over again. It's pretty natural to stay in this loop of day-to-day and near-term focus on our lives.

But how many times do we pause and give deep thought to eternity? Specifically, how often do we stop and think about what happens when we die? Likely not at all or rarely! It's a heavy subject with a lot of questions and a lot of seemingly unknowns. So it's easier just to skip the subject of our death and consequences of an unknown eternity and just keep focusing on the day-to-day.

WHAT HAPPENS WHEN I DIE?

Here is one thing that the Bible says about eternity:

> *Yet God has made everything beautiful for its own time. He has planted eternity in the human heart, but even so, people cannot see the whole scope of God's work from beginning to end.*
>
> (Ecclesiastes 3:11)

While not thinking much about dying and eternity is common, it is also a huge risk. We spend a lot of time managing our money, our house or apartment, our social calendar, and, especially, being glued to our phone, which are all going to be gone when we die. Why do we ignore eternity? Why don't we try to really understand what is going to happen when we die?

This is one of the essential questions within this book. The goal of the book is for you to take a break from day-to-day living and focus on eternity and the afterlife for a while, even though it's often a difficult and very debatable subject. All the very fleeting day-to-day things will come back very soon, but let's focus on the long term for a while!

This book is not just for people who consider themselves Christians. In fact, it is for all people of all faiths (and no faith) to evaluate and consider this collection of information.

I will use the words of the Bible as the basis for the viewpoints shared here. In fact, at least two-thirds of Bible verses quoted here are direct from the mouth of Jesus.[1]

---

[1] A Hardcover Edition of this book with Jesus' words in red is available. For more information please visit: https://www.truepotentialmedia.com/product/what-happens-when-i-die/

INTRODUCTION

I'll be using mostly the New Living Translation (NLT), one of many reliable Bible translations, unless noted otherwise. The NLT Bible translation is known for its clear, contemporary language, making it accessible to modern readers.

I am not a Biblical scholar, nor a pastor, but an average person with a profession in structural engineering and a follower of Jesus Christ. I have no formal training in theology. I'm simply using the words of Jesus and from other writers in the Bible as the guide, the evidence, for this book.

If interested, you can find more information about my life story in the appendix. This book is not intended to be my opinion, how I feel, about the Bible, but I'm simply trying to share what the Bible, mostly Jesus, clearly says about eternity, Heaven, Hell, "being good," and the two options of our fate in the afterlife.

With that, I invite you on a journey of discovery and deep thought relative to what should be the most important question of your life. Please, take a break from your phone, from the daily pressures of work and family, pause, and see what the answers are to this question! Or at least take time to evaluate this evidence, even if you have thoughts that contradict the Bible. It's definitely worth your time to consider this information!

1: The Most Important Question in Life

What is the most important question in life? Is it, "How happy can I be?" or "What can I do to make the most out of my life?" or "How can I be the best parent?" Is it, "How healthy can I keep myself to live as many years as possible on earth?" or "How can I make the most money?" How about, "How can I make my life the most impactful for the good of others?" While these are important to varying extents, they do not fit my definition of the <u>most</u> important question in life.

I would say, without a doubt, that the most important question that each of us should be asking ourselves is: ***What happens to my soul when I die?***

When I say soul, some may also refer to this as your spirit or your being. Your soul holds your mind and thoughts and intellect. Most importantly, your soul is the essential part of you that is not physical, and it will live on beyond your physical body.

WHAT HAPPENS WHEN I DIE?

The reason why this question is the most important is because it deals with eternity, which is way longer than our 60 to 100 years here on earth. Happiness and jobs will come and go, but eternity will be with us forever. What you do with your life now will determine your eternity. Let me say that again, and think deeply about it—what you do with your life now will determine your eternity!

Eternity is significant because there is a part of you that lasts forever. That is, when you die, your soul lives on forever. There is not a "lights out" event at death in which you no longer think or feel. This is clearly described in the Bible in several places, most notably the following two locations of scripture.

First, from the mouth of Jesus:

> *Jesus said, "There was a certain rich man who was splendidly clothed in purple and fine linen and who lived each day in luxury. At his gate lay a poor man named Lazarus who was covered with sores. As Lazarus lay there longing for scraps from the rich man's table, the dogs would come and lick his open sores. Finally, the poor man died and was carried by the angels to sit beside Abraham at the heavenly banquet. The rich man also died and was buried, and he went to the place of the dead. There, in torment, he saw Abraham in the far distance with Lazarus at his side. The rich man shouted, 'Father Abraham, have some pity! Send Lazarus over here to dip the tip of his finger in water and cool my tongue. I am in anguish in these flames.' But Abraham said to him, 'Son, remember that during your lifetime you had everything you wanted, and Lazarus had*

nothing. So now he is here being comforted, and you are in anguish. And besides, there is a great chasm separating us. No one can cross over to you from here, and no one can cross over to us from there.' Then the rich man said, 'Please, Father Abraham, at least send him to my father's home. For I have five brothers, and I want him to warn them so they don't end up in this place of torment.' But Abraham said, 'Moses and the prophets have warned them. Your brothers can read what they wrote.' The rich man replied, 'No, Father Abraham! But if someone is sent to them from the dead, then they will repent of their sins and turn to God.' But Abraham said, 'If they won't listen to Moses and the prophets, they won't be persuaded even if someone rises from the dead.'" (Luke 16:19-31)

Now, in these verses above it is clear that each person has their thoughts with them still and that you cannot cross from Heaven to Hell or Hell to Heaven once there.

Next, from the Apostle Paul:

What I am saying, dear brothers and sisters, is that our physical bodies cannot inherit the Kingdom of God. These dying bodies cannot inherit what will last forever. But let me reveal to you a wonderful secret. We will not all die, but we will all be transformed! It will happen in a moment, in the blink of an eye, when the last trumpet is blown. For when the trumpet sounds, those who have died will be raised to live forever. And we who are living will also be transformed. For our dying bodies must be transformed into bodies that will never die; our mortal bodies must be transformed into immortal bodies. (1 Corinthians 15:50-53)

In this passage it is clear that we will live forever in eternity. This passage is speaking to followers of Christ, thus the positivity relative to going to Heaven and getting new bodies for Heaven life. Everyone, whether going to Heaven or Hell, will maintain their soul and thought life after they die.

Going back to what I believe is the most important question in life: **What happens to my soul when I die?**

Do you agree with this question being the most important in life? If not, how important is it to you? What if you are very confident in what happens when you die and you are wrong? Are you willing to bet your life and eternity on it? This is very significant. There isn't any going back on this one. Once you die you will not be able to change your circumstances. See the text above (Luke 16:19-31), as well as:

> *Then the King will turn to those on the left and say, "Away with you, you cursed ones, into the eternal fire prepared for the devil and his demons." And they will go away into eternal punishment, but the righteous will go into eternal life.* (Matthew 25:41, 46)

If consciousness goes on forever and your ability to change your eternal position is only before you die, then finding the "right way" to prepare and live now is the most crucial thing in your life. Your life now may last 50, 70, or 100 years, but that is essentially a blip of time relative to eternity.

THE MOST IMPORTANT QUESTION IN LIFE

Eternity is hard to imagine. One visualization is to think about one grain of sand from one beach as being your life. Then take all the grains of sand from all the beaches across the world and think about a life span for each grain. Try to visualize putting each grain of sand in a line that stretches forever and each one represents about 100 years.

Here is another visualization of eternity:

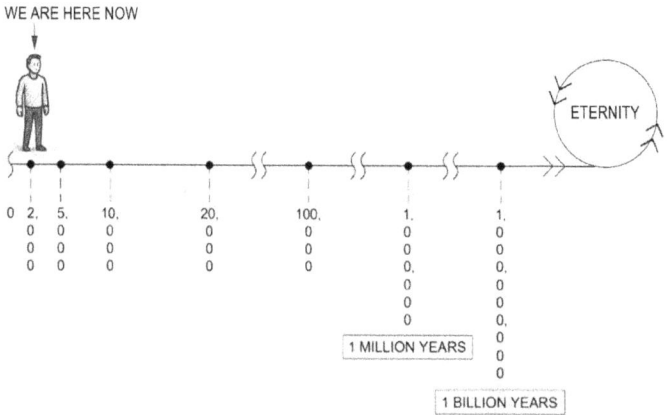

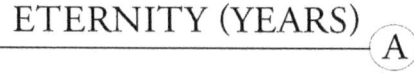

We are standing roughly around 2000 years after Christ, represented as the year 0 in the timeline above. You can see how even 3,000 years from now is still just a tiny blip on the screen of eternity, which goes on, and on and on and on! Eternity, by definition, transcends time, and that makes it conceptually challenging to express in temporal terms like a timeline. In the diagram above, eternity is represented as a never-ending circle continuing beyond what we understand as time. This visualization helps us realize the weight of eternity and your decisions. Your eternal life, after life here on earth, is so much more significant in length than your life on earth. You will have your soul, your mind, all through eternity. Therefore, understanding why you will be on one side or the other of Heaven versus Hell is so important.

2: What Does Good Enough Mean?

It is very common for people to say (or to just think) that it is relative to one's individual goodness whether they go to Heaven or not. A very common thought is, "I am a <u>good</u> person, so I am going to Heaven." Have you ever said or thought that?

When asked who doesn't make it to Heaven, it is the common thought that "very bad" people go to Hell. If that is the case, where is the line drawn? If you lie, are you still good? If you murder someone but repent of it, are you still good? If you choose to live an immoral lifestyle every week, go to church on Sunday and ask for forgiveness, yet never truly work at stopping the immoral things, are you still a "good person"?

Do only people who are in jail, or perhaps just the ones that have committed the worst acts (murderers, rapists, child abusers…) go to Hell? What percentage of people do you suppose go to Heaven and what percentage to

Hell? Are you worried about your final destination at all? How often have you really stopped to ponder this?

It is truly a slippery slope to define one's ticket to Heaven as being good enough. Think about all the decisions you make on earth relative to buying a car, buying a house, or taking on a new job. You research it, get input from others, compare and contrast, and really dig into it. And then at some point you get comfortable with the decision and move on.

But what about preparing for the biggest question of life, where you will spend eternity? Do you just "hope for the best"? It seems we should put way more research and thought into this decision than something like buying a house, right? This subject deserves our attention!

So, how good are you?

Jesus said that <u>no human</u> is good:

> *Someone came to Jesus with this question: "Teacher, what good deed must I do to have eternal life?" "Why ask me about what is good?" Jesus replied. "<u>There is only One who is good</u>. But to answer your question—if you want to receive eternal life, keep the commandments."* (Matthew 19:16-17)

When Jesus says that "there is only One that is good," he's certainly talking about the God of the Bible. And, while Jesus was fully human and fully God at the same time, He likely was talking about Himself as well, as He had a sinless life. Based on the words of Jesus above, we can now remove the argument that you or anyone else (including me, of course) are "good."

WHAT DOES 'GOOD ENOUGH' MEAN?

Furthermore, Jesus' reference to keeping the commandments has a number of layers to it. In other scripture it's clear that no one beyond Jesus kept the 10 Commandments 100% of the time while on earth—that all people have sinned in one way or another (refer to Ecclesiastes 7:20 and Romans 3:23).

Sin includes things that seem small or trivial, such as lying, pride, jealousy, bitterness, drunkenness, etc. In simple terms, **sin, according to the Bible, is anything that falls short of God's perfect standard or goes against His will**. We will never be perfect without sin, but trying to follow the 10 Commandments along with a saving faith in Jesus, as we will discuss in later chapters, is what Jesus is referring to here.

So, to answer the question, *Is "Being Good" Good Enough?* No. Being good does not get you into Heaven.

You and I will never get into Heaven by simply mustering up our own efforts to live a straight and narrow life, doing as much "good" as possible. You won't become enlightened nor go to Heaven with that alone, according to Jesus.

There are other places in the Bible that back up this statement by Jesus, that all of us are born with sin in our hearts, not born pure or sinless, including:

> *For I was born a sinner—yes, from the moment my mother conceived me.* (Psalm 51:5)

The statement above is by King David, whom God later said "he is a man after my own heart" (Acts 13:22). David ended up being very godly, but he was born a sinner, and he was not "good" by God's definition.

Also in this verse God clearly states that we are not "good" naturally:

> *And the Lord was pleased with the aroma of the sacrifice and said to himself, "I will never again curse the ground because of the human race, <u>even though everything they think or imagine is bent toward evil from childhood.</u> I will never again destroy all living things."* (Genesis 8:21)

This is God speaking after Noah and his family lived through the flood on the ark, another clear definition that we are not naturally without a sinful nature, but have it in us during childhood and at birth.

Let's look at an image that will help paint a picture of what the difference is in human potential of "goodness" versus God's perfection:

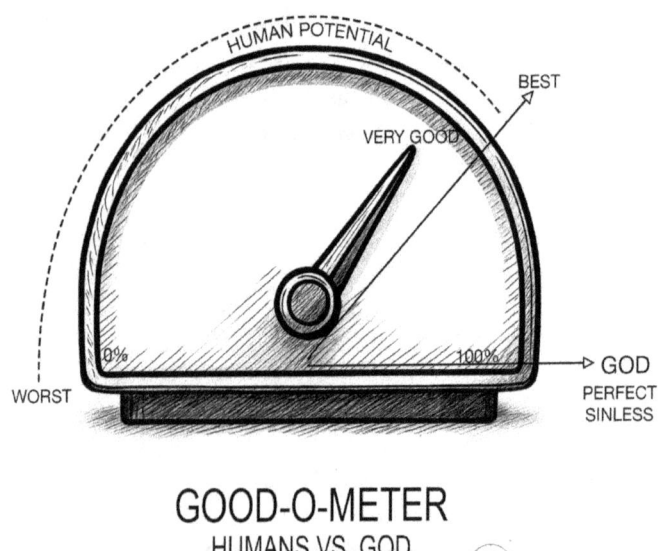

GOOD-O-METER
HUMANS VS. GOD

WHAT DOES 'GOOD ENOUGH' MEAN?

This image shows that humans are capped or limited to a certain percentage of God's perfection, that no matter what we do we can never be perfect like God, so "goodness" is just a sliding scale that never hits the mark that God demands for Heaven. That is why we need an alternate to "being good."

The common thought that being "good enough," alone, will get us into Heaven is clearly not true. So instead of betting your eternal destination on being "good enough," wouldn't you rather be 100% confident in what happens when you die?

3: Exploring Critical Questions Through Jesus' Words

Many Bibles use red letters for direct quotations of Jesus, mostly found in the four gospels of the New Testament, including Matthew, Mark, Luke, and John (and some in Acts). Why should we put so much importance on the words of Jesus?

The following are some of the most important words Jesus said regarding who He is:

> *Thomas said to Him, "Lord, we do not know where You are going, and how can we know the way?" Jesus said to him, "I am the way, the truth, and the life. No one comes to the Father except through Me. If you had known Me, you would have known My Father also; and from now on you know Him and have seen Him."* (John 14:5-7 NKJV; New King James Version/translation of the Bible)

Jesus makes it very clear that there is only one way to Heaven, through Him, and that He and the Father are one and the same relative to deity. Very bold statement by Jesus!

Jesus also acknowledged several times that He is the Son of God in other scripture (Matt 16:15-17, Matt 26:64, Mark 14:61-62, etc.).

Furthermore, here is another scripture where Jesus states who He is:

> *Then He* (Jesus) *asked them, "But who do you say I am?" Simon Peter answered, "You are the Messiah, the Son of the living God." Jesus replied, "You are blessed, Simon, son of John, because my Father in Heaven has revealed this to you. You did not learn this from any human being."* (Matthew 16:15-17)

Here Jesus acknowledges what Simon said, that Jesus is the Son of the living God. With these two verses above, Jesus is saying that He is both equal to and has the same attributes of God and that He is also the Son of God.

The goal of this section of the book is to simply use the words of Jesus to drill down on some of the questions that have been raised here so far—the most important questions in life. The point of focusing almost exclusively on the words of Jesus is supreme authenticity. People often say they can't understand the Bible and there are contradictions. There are many other books that deal with these subjects, so that discussion will be left alone here. Here's the simple point of focusing primarily on the words from Jesus:

A) If the Bible recorded things accurately, then these are the words of the one who said He is the Son of God and that He and God are one (The God of the Universe). There is overwhelming evidence that the Bible does record history correctly. I believe in the accuracy and authenticity of the Bible, and that it is the inspired word of God (written through humans), including correct translations from the original manuscripts, all guided by God.

The Bible is the most read and distributed book in the entire world, and many people died for it to share their faith. Who dies for something they don't believe in? This started with the people who knew Jesus personally when He was on Earth, and they passed it on from one generation to the next with the zeal and passion that it deserves. Many of these early Christians were willing to be put to death for this belief, and many did go through this. They did not hold their beliefs lightly.

B) If Jesus said these things, then you really only have two options on how to respond relative to believing them:

> Option 1: First, you can say that Jesus is the Son of God, that His words are truthful and have been accurately recorded and passed down through the Bible, and therefore we should heed all of them as our eternity depends on it.

> Option 2: Or, secondly, you must say that you don't believe any of the words of Jesus. In fact, you would have to say that either Jesus is a liar or He didn't say the words recorded in the Bible.

What is not an acceptable response is that you believe _some_ of the words of Jesus. Or that you believe that Jesus was a great leader or prophet or wonderful holy man, but not the Son of God. That doesn't compute, as He clearly said He was the Son of God. So, He's either that (the only Son of God and equal to God) or a liar, or these words were fabricated and accepted by people who knew Him and were willing to die for Him.

C.S. Lewis put it this way: "Christianity, if false, is of no importance, and, if true, of infinite importance. The one thing it cannot be is moderately important."[2]

We can't pick and choose which words or passages we want to believe and discount ones we don't want to believe to suit our own viewpoint. Go back to the question—are you willing to bet your eternity on your viewpoint of picking and choosing what you decide to believe relative to Jesus' words and leaving some out?

It's either all or nothing. Either Jesus is who He said He was and you believe it all, or you dismiss Jesus as a crazy person and don't accept any of His words. Going in between those two options is nonsensical and a sure way to be lost in life.

As an example, if I told you that I was the Son of God and I never sinned, then you would quickly see that isn't true and I am crazy for calling myself the Son of God. However, if Jesus didn't do anything for you to doubt His authenticity, then you should believe each and every word of His. It's all or nothing. This is essential.

---

[2] C.S. Lewis, Essay: "Christian Apologetics" (1945)

Let's dig into five key questions to understand:

What Happens When I Die?

Section 3.1: Is There Only One True God?

With people around our country and around the world having so many different religions and even different beliefs within each religion, the natural response is that there must be many ways to get to Heaven, right? It would seem like God is very mean if He has just one way, one religion, one path to truly be saved from Hell, right? Can there really be just <u>one</u> real path to getting to Heaven? Well, let's examine what Jesus said about this:

> *Jesus came and told his disciples, "I have been given <u>all authority</u> in Heaven and on earth."* (Matthew 28:18)

> *And He took a cup of wine and gave thanks to God for it. He gave it to them and said, "Each of you drink from it, for this is my blood, which confirms the covenant between God and his people. It is poured out as a sacrifice <u>to forgive the sins of many</u>."* (Matthew 26:27-28)

Furthermore, after Jesus was crucified and His followers were looking for Him, two angels appeared at the tomb where the stone had been rolled away from the entrance to where they laid Jesus a couple days prior, and the angels said:

> *He isn't here! He is risen from the dead! Remember what he told you back in Galilee, that the Son of Man must be betrayed into the hands of sinful men*

and be crucified, and that he would rise again on the third day. (Luke 24:6-7)

Then for proof of His bodily resurrection after His crucifixion, Jesus came to the disciples just days later and said the following:

Look at my hands. Look at my feet. You can see that it's really me. Touch me and make sure that I am not a ghost, because ghosts don't have bodies, as you see that I do. (Luke 24:39)

However, one of the disciples was not with them the first time Jesus appeared to them. This is how that interaction came about:

One of the twelve disciples, Thomas (nicknamed 'doubting Thomas'), was not with the others when Jesus came. They told him, "We have seen the Lord!" But he replied, "I won't believe it unless I see the nail wounds in his hands, put my fingers into them, and place my hand into the wound in his side." Eight days later the disciples were together again, and this time Thomas was with them. The doors were locked; but suddenly, as before, Jesus was standing among them. "Peace be with you," he said. Then he said to Thomas, "Put your finger here, and look at my hands. Put your hand into the wound in my side. Don't be faithless any longer. Believe!" "My Lord and my God!" Thomas exclaimed. Then Jesus told him, "You believe because you have seen me. Blessed are those who believe without seeing me."
(John 20:24-29)

In the previous verses, Jesus is establishing that He is the one that forgives sins, that He has all authority over Heaven and Earth, and that He did actually rise from the dead. These are all strong and bold statements that point to Jesus as being the one and only true God. Let's also examine a couple of the major miracles Jesus did:

Jesus had control over nature:

> *When Jesus woke up, he rebuked the wind and said to the waves, "Silence! Be still!" Suddenly the wind stopped, and there was a great calm.* (Mark 4:39)

Jesus also raised three people from the dead and clearly did this with His position as the Son of God. Here is the recounting of one of these:

> *"Roll the stone aside," Jesus told them. But Martha, the dead man's sister, protested, "Lord, he has been dead for four days. The smell will be terrible." Jesus responded, "Didn't I tell you that you would see God's glory if you believe?" So they rolled the stone aside. Then Jesus looked up to heaven and said, "Father, thank you for hearing me. You always hear me, but I said it out loud for the sake of all these people standing here, so that they will believe you sent me." Then Jesus shouted, "Lazarus, come out!" And the dead man came out, his hands and feet bound in graveclothes, his face wrapped in a headcloth. Jesus told them, "Unwrap him and let him go!"*
> (John 11:39-44)

Jesus could control nature, He could raise people from the dead, and He could heal people. All lending to the evidence that He is God.

Next let's look at the most specific words from Jesus that answer the question asked in this section *(Is There Only One True God?)*:

> *Jesus told him, "I am the way, the truth, and the life. <u>No one</u> can come to the Father* (God) *except through me. If you had really known me, you would know who my Father is. From now on, you do know Him and have seen Him!"* (John 14:6-7)

This obviously puts Jesus' position at odds with the very common mentality that there are multiple ways to get into Heaven, many religions that get you to the same place, and everyone is free to choose their own path.

Jesus is clearly saying that there is only one way, through Him and His ways. If Jesus' words are true here, then everyone outside of what He says is going to Hell. Again, this is the time I'd like to point out that it is nonsensical to pick just some of the things that Jesus said as truth and discard other things.

Jesus is either all that He says He is (the Messiah, the Savior, the one that covers over our sin, the one who is the same as God, and the only way to Heaven) or He's totally a false prophet that you can't believe anything from. It's one or the other; we can't pick and choose just some of His words to believe, as that is the same as saying you don't believe Him as the one and only true Lord.

Let's look a bit further into the verses after the one above to give even more context to what Jesus is saying to the disciples and to us:

Philip said, "Lord, show us the Father, and we will be satisfied." Jesus replied, "Have I been with you all this time, Philip, and yet you still don't know who I am? Anyone who has seen me has seen the Father! So why are you asking me to show him to you? Don't you believe that I am in the Father and the Father is in me? The words I speak are not my own, but my Father who lives in me does his work through me. Just believe that I am in the Father and the Father is in me. Or at least believe because of the work you have seen me do." (John 14:8-11)

If we pull together all these words from Jesus' own lips, then it is very clear that He is the only true God and the only way to get to Heaven! There is no ambiguity here. As stated before, my aim is to let Jesus' own words speak for themselves. Therefore, we must listen closely to what Jesus says and do what He says to do, as our eternity is at stake.

Section 3.2: How Good Are We Really?

It is extremely common for people to think to themselves, "I'm a good person." We often self-assess and come away feeling that we aren't perfect, that we do a few things wrong, but in general we are "good people." What is the definition of "being good"?

If we surveyed thousands of people, asking what the definition of "being good" is, then there will definitely be a large variation of answers, but a fair amount of commonality too. Let's go to the current voice of authority (ha!), ChatGPT, and see what it has to say:

Question: "What is the most common definition of being a good human being?"

ChatGPT Answer: "The most common definition of being a good human being often revolves around traits such as kindness, empathy, honesty, integrity, compassion, and respect for others. It's about treating others the way you would want to be treated, being considerate of others' feelings, and acting in a way that contributes positively to the well-being of individuals and society as a whole. This definition can vary slightly depending on cultural, religious, and personal beliefs, but these core values are generally universal."

So now that we have a general thought on what the world believes "being good" is, what did Jesus say about this?

> *"Why do you call me good?" Jesus asked. "Only God is truly good."* (Mark 10:18)

This is a quick and direct retort to common thought that most people are good; however, we are not "good people" according to Jesus.

In fact, the Bible clearly teaches that we are not "good" by human nature, but we are actually sinful (bad) by our nature:

> *For I was born a sinner—yes, from the moment my mother conceived me.* (Psalm 51:5)

> *The human heart is the most deceitful of all things, and desperately wicked. Who really knows how bad it is?* (Jeremiah 17:9)

Wow, that sounds extreme. However, here are more words from Jesus to confirm the Old Testament verses above:

> *And then he added, "It is what comes from inside that defiles you. For from within, out of a person's heart, come evil thoughts, sexual immorality, theft, murder, adultery, greed, wickedness, deceit, lustful desires, envy, slander, pride, and foolishness. <u>All these vile things come from within; they are what defile you.</u>"* (Mark 7:20-23)

Of course, this doesn't mean that every person has or acts on these thoughts, but we all have some form of ungodliness in us and we do these things in our lives (lie, have pride, don't love others as ourselves, cheat in small or big ways, etc.). As a human race, all of these ungodly or sinful things listed are within our societies.

Furthermore, Jesus says:

> *You fathers—if your children ask for a fish, do you give them a snake instead? Or if they ask for an egg, do you give them a scorpion? Of course not! So if you <u>sinful people</u> know how to give good gifts to your children, how much more will your heavenly Father give the Holy Spirit to those who ask him.* (Luke 11:11-13)

Note that Jesus calls us sinful/evil by nature, not good by nature, opposite of what is commonly thought here on earth.

All these verses line up to tell us that we are <u>not</u> good by human nature and none of us lives anything near to a sinless life. Does God judge on a sliding scale? Not at all! It's either 100% one way or another—either we've sinned at least once or in small ways (and thus we have broken God's law), or we are perfect and sinless (which no one is).

We are all sinful at birth and there is only one way to become holy in God's eyes. Saying that we are good and, therefore, we will go to Heaven is not anywhere close to accurate in God's definition. We all sin and fall short of the glory of God. In fact, there is only one way to Heaven, as we read above, and we'll find out more on the "how" in later chapters.

Section 3.3: What Does Hell Look Like?

It is really easy to not feel the impact of how long eternity is nor how terrible Hell is. It's very natural to not give these two things much thought at all. Who wants to dwell on what Hell will be like? We are much more interested in other things and that can wait or not ever really be thought of, right?

However, it's critical to answering the question, "What happens to my soul when I die?" We must dig in and understand this place called Hell, not avoid it. Let's go to the most trusted resource, Jesus, to hear what Hell is like. Jesus spoke more about Hell than He did about Heaven, and here are some of His descriptions below:

> *"If your hand causes you to sin, cut it off. It's better to enter eternal life with only one hand than to go into the <u>unquenchable fires of Hell</u> with two*

hands...<u>where the maggots never die and the fire never goes out.</u>" (Mark 9:43-48)

Now, there can be a lot of discussion about really cutting off your hand (or other parts discussed in this full verse); however, it's clear what the description of Hell is. It has an unquenchable fire, and maggots that never die. What a horrible place to exist, hour after hour, day after day.

Furthermore:

> *"Just as the weeds are sorted out and burned in the fire, so it will be at the end of the world. The Son of Man* (Jesus) *will send his angels, and they will remove from his Kingdom everything that causes sin and all who do evil. And the angels will throw them into the fiery furnace, <u>where there will be weeping and gnashing of teeth</u>. Then the righteous will shine like the sun in their Father's Kingdom. Anyone with ears to hear should listen and understand!"* (Matthew 13:40-43)

In these verses above it says there will be "weeping and gnashing of teeth" in Hell due to the fiery furnace, unquenchable fires, and no hope. This reinforces the earlier discussion that people will have their thoughts, their conscious self, and it won't be a "lights out" moment. There will be pain and agony and it won't end.

Let's review again a verse we looked at early on in this book:

> *Jesus said, "There was a certain rich man who was splendidly clothed in purple and fine linen and who lived each day in luxury. At his gate lay a poor man*

named Lazarus who was covered with sores. As Lazarus lay there longing for scraps from the rich man's table, the dogs would come and lick his open sores. Finally, the poor man died and was carried by the angels to sit beside Abraham at the heavenly banquet. The rich man also died and was buried, and he went to the place of the dead. There, <u>in torment</u>, he saw Abraham in the far distance with Lazarus at his side. The rich man shouted, 'Father Abraham, have some pity! Send Lazarus over here to dip the tip of his finger in water and cool my tongue. <u>I am in anguish in these flames.</u>' But Abraham said to him, 'Son, remember that during your lifetime you had everything you wanted, and Lazarus had nothing. So now he is here being comforted, and you are in anguish. And besides, there is a great chasm separating us. No one can cross over to you from here, and no one can cross over to us from there.' Then the rich man said, 'Please, Father Abraham, at least send him to my father's home. For I have five brothers, and I want him to warn them so they don't end up in this place of torment.' But Abraham said, 'Moses and the prophets have warned them. Your brothers can read what they wrote.' The rich man replied, 'No, Father Abraham! But if someone is sent to them from the dead, then they will repent of their sins and turn to God.' But Abraham said, 'If they won't listen to Moses and the prophets, they won't be persuaded even if someone rises from the dead.'" (Luke 16:19-31)

These words from Jesus give us a very unsettling view of Hell. From this and the previous verses, we see that Jesus describes Hell as:

- continual torment
- nothing pleasant will be given to those in Hell
- no way out or to change the situation
- never ending

It is clear that dying is not a "lights out" event, but it is a major change from what we are living now. We are headed for a significant change to either Heaven or Hell when we die and we must be ready. God gives everyone an option to avoid Hell, as we will discuss more in later chapters.

There are a ton of questions that center on these statements by Jesus. One very common and understandable question is "How can a loving God allow this, for people to be tormented forever?" This is a tough question for us to understand.

My aim is to point to what Jesus said about these things. However, it seems the answer is, God is love and God is also just. He wants everyone to be saved from Hell, but He gives every person on earth the choice to call on Him (the one true God), to trust Him, or not. Each person is given the opportunity to feel the tugging of the Holy Spirit and answer it, or not.

Note that the **Holy Spirit** of the Bible is often described as **God's active presence** here on Earth, guiding and empowering believers.

Many things of God are just beyond the human mind and this would be one of them, but it is the truth.

Section 3.4: What Does Heaven Look Like?

With the grim view of Hell just completed, let's look at the total opposite—what it will be like to be in Heaven.

Believe it or not, there are actually a few things that are the same about Heaven and Hell:

1. Both Heaven and Hell (Lake of Fire/Hades) last for eternity.

2. The inhabitants of each location will never leave that place nor change from one location to the other.

3. The inhabitants of each place will have eternal consciousness and eternal lives.

4. There will be a constant leader over each location—God in Heaven and Satan in Hell.

Now, the similarities end there.

Heaven is often depicted as angels with wings sitting on clouds playing harps. It's kind of a goofy depiction that gives some sense of peacefulness but also thoughts of boredom. But what exactly does Jesus and the Bible say about Heaven? Will the inhabitants have bodies anything like ours now? What would you do with all that time? What will relationships be like? Will we get to eat great food? What's the big draw?

The Bible says quite a bit about Heaven. It clears up most of these questions and more, but it certainly doesn't answer all questions. Furthermore, in our current limited human state we really can't imagine the true greatness of

Heaven and not everything has been 100% clearly laid out in the Bible—some things will remain a mystery until we are there, as pointed out in this scripture:

> *That is what the Scriptures mean when they say, "No eye has seen, no ear has heard, and no mind has imagined what God has prepared for those who love him."* (1 Corinthians 2:9)

Wow, Heaven is beyond what we can even imagine! That is exciting to think about. This verse also puts to rest the stories of modern-day people dying briefly, coming back to life and telling us what Heaven is like. I strongly recommend not entertaining those stories, we should rely on the fullness and authenticity of the Bible, alone!

If we dive into some verses of the Bible, we can start to gain a new level of understanding and appreciation of Heaven.

The single most critical point about the greatness of Heaven is this: we will be in the presence of the Lord God, our maker and the maker of the universe, forever! The one who loves us in a way that is way beyond human love and one that wants us to be with Him forever! This most important thing about Heaven will be fully realized when we are there and it's often hard to grasp this while we are here on earth, but let's try!

Here are some things that Jesus shared with us about Heaven:

> *Jesus came and told his disciples, "I have been given all authority in heaven and on earth."* (Matthew 28:18)

Jesus will rule and reign in Heaven and He has authority to decide who goes there.

> *Then the King will turn to those on the left and say, "Away with you, you cursed ones, into the eternal fire prepared for the devil and his demons." And they will go away into eternal punishment, but the righteous will go into eternal life* (Heaven). (Matthew 25:41, 46)

Here is the certainty that our consciousness and spirit will last forever—Jesus calls life in Heaven (and Hell) eternal many times.

> *And just as my Father has granted me a Kingdom* (Heaven), *I now grant you the right to eat and drink at my table in my Kingdom. And you will sit on thrones, judging the twelve tribes of Israel.* (Luke 22:29-30)

We will have a close loving continual relationship with Jesus and we'll have duties/roles/jobs to do. We also get to eat! Sharing a meal is an essential part of relationship building, and personal enjoyment, of course!

> *Don't let your hearts be troubled. Trust in God, and trust also in me. There is more than enough room in my Father's home* (Heaven). *If this were not so, would I have told you that I am going to prepare a place for you? When everything is ready, I will come and get you, so that you will always be with me where I am.* (John 14:1-3)

This verse goes back to the main point of Heaven—we will be with the God of the universe, the Trinity, in a close loving relationship. This concept of the Trinity means that **God exists as one God in three distinct persons: God the Father, God the Son (Jesus), and God the Holy Spirit**, all equally divine. We will be with Jesus, who died for our sins to give us the opportunity for eternity in Heaven.

We can't imagine the depth of His love and what it will be like to be in His presence, but we can try! And it's clear here that there is plenty of room for anyone to make it into Heaven and that God is specifically preparing a place for us! That is so enticing to think about a new perfect home and life being prepared for us.

Another related verse from the Old Testament of the Bible, the wisdom book of Psalms:

> *No wonder my heart is glad, and I rejoice. My body rests in safety. For you will not leave my soul among the dead or allow your holy one to rot in the grave. You will show me the way of life, <u>granting me the joy of your presence and the pleasures of living with you forever</u>.* (Psalm 16:9-11)

What more could we ask for than this: "joy of God's presence" and "pleasures forevermore"? This isn't just so much better than the alternative (Hell), but radically better than our current existence on Earth. Can our lives on earth be fun, exciting, rewarding, and peaceful at times? Yes, and those are gifts right from the hand of God. He's giving us a small taste of what Heaven will be like. However, Heaven is so much more.

In life now, do you ever get angry, depressed, sad? Are you ever worried about the future, about your kids, about your spouse, your loved ones? These feelings will all be gone when in Heaven and we will have constant joy!

What about our bodies in Heaven? Let's look at these verses for input:

> *But we are citizens of heaven, where the Lord Jesus Christ lives. And we are eagerly waiting for him to return as our Savior. He will take our weak mortal bodies and change them into glorious bodies <u>like his own</u>, using the same power with which he will bring everything under his control.* (Philippians 3:20-21)
>
> *...we will not be spirits without bodies.* (2 Corinthians 5:3)
>
> *It is the same way with the resurrection of the dead. Our earthly bodies are planted in the ground when we die, but they will be raised to live forever. They are buried as natural human bodies, but they will be raised as spiritual bodies. For just as there are natural bodies, there are also spiritual bodies.* (1 Corinthians 15:42-44)

Furthermore, we can look at Jesus' time on earth after His resurrection as a good view into what our heavenly bodies and relationships will be like, as described in the four Gospels and the Book of Acts (and in the Philippians verse above). Jesus lived on earth for 40 days after His death and resurrection, before His ascension to Heaven, and He interacted with His disciples and others (including 500 people at one time). This gives us good input on what we can expect for our bodies in Heaven.

Jesus' resurrected body looked a lot like His earthly body (but without the possibility of decay). He ate food with

His loved ones. They could touch Him, so He wasn't a ghost, but physical.

Beyond that Jesus could do some things that we cannot do as humans now, like teleporting from one location to another in an instant and walk through walls. Also, He could change His appearance to look like someone else. I'm doubting that we'll have all these capabilities, as He was/is God. However, it's clear from all these verses that we will have spiritual bodies very similar to that of Jesus.

In addition to having great activities to keep us busy in Heaven, what we do on earth now will affect how we live in Heaven:

> *Store your treasures in Heaven, where moths and rust cannot destroy, and thieves do not break in and steal.* (Matthew 6:20)

Therefore, once we have a trusting/saving relationship with Jesus, our focus should be to do God's will here on Earth, as what we receive in Heaven depends on our actions here (however, being saved is not based on our good works, as we will discuss more in the next section).

Note what the Bible says about whose account of Heaven we should believe:

> *No one has ever gone to heaven and returned. But the Son of Man has come down from heaven.* (John 3:13)

With this, should we believe people who say they were temporarily brought to Heaven during a near-death experience and write a book about it or post it on social media? These stories often sound really good. However, these stories can vary widely and who's to know what is real? Instead of relying on people, who are frail and sinful from birth, it's much more reliable to believe in what the Bible says about Heaven, including words right from the mouth of Jesus!

What if you never worried again? What if you were never sad again? Let's look at what the Book of Revelation, the last book of the New Testament of the Bible, tells us, as revealed by an angel talking to John the Apostle.

First, let's look at the introduction to the Book of Revelation:

> *This is a revelation <u>from Jesus Christ</u>, which God gave him to show his servants the events that must soon take place. He sent an angel to present this revelation to his servant John, who faithfully reported everything he saw. <u>This is his report of the word of God and the testimony of Jesus Christ.</u> God blesses the one who reads the words of this prophecy to the church, and he blesses all who listen to its message and obey what it says, for the time is near.* (Revelation 1:1-3)

Now let's look at some verses about our future relationship with God in Heaven:

> *I heard a loud shout from the throne, saying, "Look, God's home is now among his people! He will live with them, and they will be his people. God himself will be with them. He will wipe every tear from their eyes, and there will be no more death or sorrow or crying or pain. All these things are gone forever." And the one sitting on the throne said, "Look, I am mak-*

ing everything new!" And then he said to me, "Write this down, for what I tell you is trustworthy and true." And he also said, "It is finished! I am the Alpha and the Omega—the Beginning and the End. To all who are thirsty I will give freely from the springs of the water of life. All who are victorious will inherit all these blessings, and I will be their God, and they will be my children." (Revelation 21:3-7)

These verses describe the essential difference between Heaven and Hell. Hell is wailing and gnashing of teeth (eternal absence from the Lord). Heaven is being in the presence of the Almighty—joy, peace and wonderful pleasures forevermore.

Anyone given this clear choice between these two would choose the latter—but why do people not often pursue God to make sure of this as our main goal in life? Many people think they are going to Heaven, feeling "I'm fine" as is, without ever truly reaching out to God. Go back to the section on "how good are we really?" We are not "fine" the way we are born; something must happen, something must change to secure our soul in Heaven. We will discuss this more in the next chapters.

Further in the Book of Revelation, the angel tells of what God calls the "New Jerusalem," the description of the final Heaven that awaits us:

And he carried me away in the Spirit to a mountain great and high, and showed me the Holy City, Jerusalem, coming down out of heaven from God. It shone with the glory of God, and its brilliance was like that of a very precious jewel, like a jasper, clear as crystal. It had a great, high wall with twelve gates, and with twelve angels at the gates. On the gates were written the names of the twelve tribes of Israel. There were three gates on the east, three on the north, three on the south and three on the west. The wall of the city had twelve foundations, and on them were the names of the twelve apostles of the Lamb.

The angel who talked with me had a measuring rod of gold to measure the city, its gates and its walls. The city was laid out like a square, as long as it was wide. He measured the city with the rod and found it to be 12,000 stadia in length, and as wide and high as it is long. The angel measured the wall using human measurement, and it was 144 cubits thick. The wall was made of jasper, and the city of pure gold, as pure as glass. The foundations of the city walls were decorated with every kind of precious stone. The first foundation was jasper, the second sapphire, the third agate, the fourth emerald, the fifth onyx, the sixth ruby, the seventh chrysolite, the eighth beryl, the ninth topaz, the tenth turquoise, the eleventh jacinth, and the twelfth amethyst. The twelve gates were twelve pearls, each gate made of a single pearl. The great street of the city was of gold, as pure as transparent glass.

I did not see a temple in the city, because the Lord God Almighty and the Lamb are its temple. <u>The city does not need the sun or the moon to shine on it, for the glory of God gives it light, and the Lamb is its lamp</u>. The nations will walk by its light, and the kings of the earth will bring their splendor into it. On no day will its gates ever be shut, <u>for there</u>

<u>will be no night there</u>. The glory and honor of the nations will be brought into it. <u>Nothing impure will ever enter it</u>, nor will anyone who does what is shameful or deceitful, <u>but only those whose names are written in the Lamb's book of life.</u> (Revelation 21:10-27 NIV; New International Version/translation of the Bible)

Wow! What an amazing place awaits all who are saved by the blood of Jesus Christ, who have their names written in the Lamb's Book of Life (those who have a saving faith/trust in Jesus)! Now, with our human minds we often want to question something so specific like this and say, really, that can't really be what Heaven is like! But we are humans, and this is God's word, and that is where faith comes in.

We need to put our faith in something—us, Jesus Christ, or something else, right? Where do we feel the most reliable answer is? The Bible's words and the history that has played out since Jesus walked the earth certainly does have strong evidence, more than anything else I've seen!

Using the Book of Revelation, the other books of the Bible noted here, and the words of Jesus himself in the Gospels and the Book of Acts, here is a general summary of what to expect in Heaven:

1. No more tears, no more sadness, no more sorrow

2. No more death, no more sickness, no more health issues at all

3. We get a new immortal body that is similar to the one Jesus had while walking on earth after His resurrection

4. Heaven will not have night, but it will shine continuously from the light of God. So really no normal concept of time that we have now, as there will not be a day then night, but it will be a continuum of light-filled living

5. There will not be a physical temple (or church or worship building), as God is the Living Temple and we'll be in His presence every day

6. We will get enjoyment out of our work/duties and will see (and use) the results of our labor

7. We will not get bored; we'll continually grow and learn and enjoy everything we do

8. There will be nothing unholy allowed to enter Heaven

9. Animals of all types will get along and along with humans—no more prey

10. The only people there are ones whose names are written in the Lamb's Book of Life

11. We'll have joy and fullness of the Lord's exceeding riches for all eternity

Now that sounds too good to be true, doesn't it? Well, it's not. It is true. We all need to stop and take time to let this sink in.

Eternity in Heaven or Hell is where we all will spend 99.99999999999999% of our total time with our soul/consciousness. Put another way, it will be eternal life with God or eternal punishment/torment. See the visualization of eternity on page 15 (Figure A).

Stop and really let that sink in. Our life on earth is but a small blip on the timescale of eternity. It's so easy and common to think that our life here is so important. However, in reality, our life beyond this earth is so overwhelmingly long that we really need to think about it much more.

We must think about "life" beyond death. For whatever pain and struggles or whatever fun and cherished time we have here on earth, it's so momentary. Our lives here are like one second of time compared to the length of eternity. Are you ready to bet your eternity on your current beliefs? Are you 100% confident where you are going?

Heaven is so inviting and so rewarding and beyond what these words here could even try to depict! Now we need to find out with certainty how we get in the Lamb's Book of Life (Revelation 21:27) to secure our spot in Heaven!

Section 3.5: Who Is Going to Hell and Who Is Going to Heaven?

Now the discussion gets very difficult. Talking about what Hell is like is one thing, but talking about who is going there is another. The only thing to stand on here is what the Bible specifically says about this and not what individuals think about each other. It is, and will always be, only God who knows which direction each person is headed.

This is a good place to restate the commonly held belief of many people who identify themselves as "Christians" and many others in other religions or in no religion at all.

That is, many people think "good people" go to Heaven and "bad people" go to Hell, and the list of what qualifies as 'bad' is usually only the worst offenders in society. Under this viewpoint of "only really bad people" go to Hell, where is the line drawn?

Many people think that people who have murdered or have raped or who are pedophiles will for sure be in Hell, right? But what if you steal from another person or from a store or your employer—does that send you to Hell? What if you don't physically steal from your employer but you often waste time on personal activities and over-report your work hours, effectively lying? If you lie to your spouse or good friend, do you go to Hell? What if you cheat on your spouse, do you go to Hell? If you make fun of other people, do you go to Hell? Where is the line drawn?

This is a very slippery slope and a viewpoint you don't want to be holding onto. Defining people as "good" or "bad" just doesn't work.

Therefore, let's hear the words from Jesus himself:

> *Jesus told him, "I am the way, the truth, and the life. <u>No one</u> can come to the Father except through me. If you had <u>really</u> known me, you would know who my Father is. From now on, you do know him and have seen him!"* (John 14:6-7)

Wow, this is a bold statement in today's world. First, Jesus is saying that He and God are the same when it comes to us getting to Heaven. Second, right here Jesus is stating in black and white terms that there is no other way to Heaven except through Him and what He has taught about true Christianity.

According to this, trying any other way, including those who put their faith in other religions, including Judaism, Islam, Buddhism, Hinduism, etc. (or no religion), these people are all missing out on Heaven and going to Hell for eternity according to Jesus. Why? Because they haven't put their faith and trust in Jesus, but in other things. I realize these claims can sound exclusive and offensive, but my aim is to let Jesus' own words speak for themselves, not my opinion. Furthermore, the God of the Bible wants everyone to go to Heaven, but it's clear that we need to take some specific action steps to fulfill that desire of His.

That is a sobering statement by Jesus. It obviously makes people question Jesus and this statement, saying that there is no way it can be true. Many people will state that there is no way that a loving God would give such a narrow way to Heaven. The Bible is clear that God's justice and holiness require that sin be judged, but His love moved Him to provide the solution in Jesus.

Look at all of Jesus' life and take everything into account and ask: Is He who He says He is? Or is He a liar? It is really all or nothing with Jesus. You can't take some of His words and not others. He is either fully who He says He is, or He is not a god or prophet or wise person, as He would have had to lie if you don't believe John 14:6-7.

Let's dig into this more, with these words by Jesus:

> *"For this is how God loved the world: He gave his one and only Son, <u>so that everyone who **believes** in</u>*

*<u>him will not perish but have eternal life</u>. God sent his Son into the world not to judge the world, but to save the world through him. There is no judgment against anyone who believes in him. <u>But anyone who does not **believe** in him has already been judged</u> for not believing in God's one and only Son. And the judgment is based on this fact: God's light came into the world, but people loved the darkness more than the light, for their actions were evil."* (John 3:16-19)

And the apostle Paul reaffirms this significant truth later in the Bible:

Anyone who denies the Son doesn't have the Father, either. But anyone who acknowledges the Son has the Father also. (1 John 2:23)

These verses continue the same theme, that Jesus is the one way to Heaven. According to Jesus and the Bible, there is no other way. Just as importantly, we need to dig into what it means to "believe" in Jesus through the next several verses, according to Jesus.

Jesus called a little child to him and put the child among them. Then he said, "I tell you the truth, <u>unless you turn from your sins and become like little children</u>, you will never get into the Kingdom of Heaven." (Matthew 18:3)

One may ask, how do I become like a little child? I believe it is being humble and accepting Jesus' words as they are, by faith, like the way children often accept the things they are told by adults.

So far, we are told to "believe," "turn from our sins," and "become like little children." Here is more guidance from Jesus:

> *There was a man named Nicodemus, a Jewish religious leader who was a Pharisee. After dark one evening, he came to speak with Jesus. "Rabbi," he said, "we all know that God has sent you to teach us. Your miraculous signs are evidence that God is with you." Jesus replied, "I tell you the truth, <u>unless you are born again</u>, you cannot see the Kingdom of God* (Heaven)*." "What do you mean?" exclaimed Nicodemus. "How can an old man go back into his mother's womb and be born again?" Jesus replied, "I assure you, <u>no one</u> can enter the Kingdom of God without <u>being born of water and the Spirit</u>. Humans can reproduce only human life, <u>but the Holy Spirit gives birth to spiritual life</u>. So don't be surprised when I say, 'You must be born again.'"*
> (John 3:1-7)

So Jesus doesn't list any specific sins that must be avoided, but He says you must be "born again," born of the Holy Spirit and born of water. He didn't say you need to be "good." He didn't say we must say a special prayer or do a certain ritual. Adding this to the items above (believe/trust in Jesus only, turn from our sins, believe like little children, and be born of the Holy Spirit) is the essence of what we need to do to guarantee our place in Heaven. And, to clarify, turning from our sins isn't what gets us saved, but it is a result and action that naturally evolves after we have truly believed in Jesus. Furthermore, "being born of the Spirit" is something that happens to us, from God, when we fully trust in Jesus to cover our sins.

In essence, **to be "born again" means receiving a new, spiritual life from God through the Holy Spirit**, marked by a heart-level belief and trust in Jesus.

Essentially, it's us believing and trusting in Jesus that He died for our sins and paid the way for us to go to Heaven, period! In the next chapters we will pull this together with the rest of the critical things here and talk more about the process of being born again, born of the Holy Spirit. Furthermore, it's important to know that this process of being born again wipes away all sins: past, present, and future.

Regarding "born of water" in the verses above, there is some debate on what exactly this means. The most commonly held belief is that "born of water" simply means to be born of human descent, the water referring to a woman's amniotic sac, which normally breaks before birth.

On the other hand, some scholars believe this refers to a passage in the Old Testament, way before Jesus was on earth. In Ezekiel 36:25-27, the Prophet Ezekiel talks about God "sprinkling clean water on you," as part of the born-again process.

Either way, this is not something that any person has to seek out to be truly saved; it's not an extra step that has to be accomplished. With that, I believe that our part is to believe and trust in the one who died for our sins (Jesus), then the process of conversion happens and we are both "born again" and "born of water."

Note that it is said elsewhere in the New Testament to "be baptized and then obey," including directly from Jesus in what is called the Great Commission:

Jesus came and told his disciples, "I have been given all authority in heaven and on earth. Therefore, go and make disciples of all the nations, baptizing them in the name of the Father and the Son and the Holy Spirit. Teach these new disciples to obey all the commands I have given you. And be sure of this: I am with you always, even to the end of the age." (Matthew 28:18-20)

So we are told that <u>after</u> conversion (after we become disciples/followers of Jesus) we should be baptized, as an outward sign to others of our new-found belief. And any baptism <u>prior</u> to this doesn't do the same thing or count in the same way—it's after we have been born again. Baby baptism, or other baptisms alone, prior to a heartfelt decision to believe/trust in Jesus as your Lord and Savior, doesn't align with scripture, and therefore do not get you to Heaven, from everything I understand from the Bible.

Furthermore, you don't have to be baptized to be saved (but you should do it!). A great example of this is when Jesus was on the cross and one of the two thieves beside Him came to true belief in Jesus:

But the other criminal protested, "Don't you fear God even when you have been sentenced to die? We deserve to die for our crimes, but this man hasn't done anything wrong." Then he said, "Jesus, remember me when you come into your Kingdom." And Jesus replied, "I assure you, <u>today</u> you will be with me in paradise." (Luke 23:40-43)

This is a great example and proof of God/Jesus knowing people's true motivation of their heart. This thief did not say a long prayer with certain words (he didn't pray at all, or not recorded) and he wasn't baptized, and he didn't get to Heaven by "being good," but he had true belief, faith and trust in Jesus, and Jesus saw that and saved him on the spot!

This verse makes it clear that simple faith like this man, who apparently did something very bad to be hung on a cross, was enough to save him in that instant. Many people today would assume that this "bad criminal" could never go to Heaven, but that clearly is not the case.

Wow, it's refreshing to see an example of someone being saved without going through a ton of steps that many people feel are needed to go to Heaven. It's all about true trust and belief in the Son of God for what He did for us on the cross. Furthermore, this is how I believe everyone before Jesus was judged by God, by their response to the Scriptures and the motivation of their heart relative to God, which only God knows.

Let's look into more words from Jesus about Heaven:

> *Here is another story Jesus told: "The Kingdom of Heaven is like a farmer who planted <u>good seed</u> in his field. But that night as the workers slept, his enemy came and <u>planted weeds</u> among the wheat, then slipped away. When the crop began to grow and produce grain, the weeds also grew. The farmer's workers went to him and said, 'Sir, the field where you planted that good seed is full of weeds! Where did they come from?' 'An enemy has done this!' the farmer exclaimed. 'Should we pull out the weeds?' they asked. 'No,' he replied, 'you'll uproot the wheat if you do. Let both grow together until the harvest. Then I will tell the harvesters to sort out the weeds,*

tie them into bundles, and burn them, and to put the wheat in the barn." (Matthew 13:24-30)

Thanks to Jesus' disciples we get deeper insight:

Then, leaving the crowds outside, Jesus went into the house. His disciples said, "Please explain to us the story of the weeds in the field." Jesus replied, "The Son of Man is the farmer who plants the good seed. The field is the world, and the good seed represents the people of the Kingdom (Heaven). *The weeds are the people who belong to the evil one. The enemy who planted the weeds among the wheat is the devil. The harvest is the end of the world, and the harvesters are the angels. <u>Just as the weeds are sorted out and burned in the fire, so it will be at the end of the world.</u> The Son of Man will send his angels, and they will remove from his Kingdom everything that causes sin and all who do evil. And the angels will throw them into the fiery furnace, where there will be weeping and gnashing of teeth. Then the righteous will shine like the sun in their Father's Kingdom. Anyone with ears to hear should listen and understand!"* (Matthew 13:36-43)

OK, it's clear that Jesus says some will go to Heaven and some to Hell. But what does "all who do evil" mean? In previous chapters I've pointed out that all of us sin and fall short of the glory of God. There is no one without sin, except Jesus.

I believe the statement above "all who do evil" refers to people who are <u>not</u> born-again, according to Jesus' definition above. It's all of us until we are converted and start a new life led by Jesus. The rest of the verses from Jesus

WHAT HAPPENS WHEN I DIE?

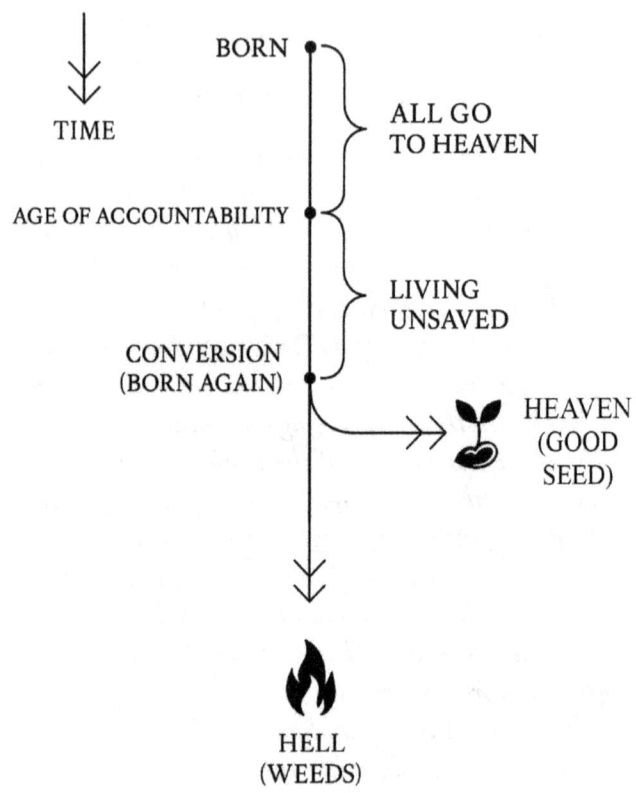

MATTHEW 13:24-30 & 13:36-43 —C

and the New Testament supports this conclusion. Image "C" above, gives a visual representation of this and John 3:1-7 (and related verses in the previous few pages).

The visual on the opposite page identifies that we are all born sinful, that there is a period of grace for children to some age, then those who trust in Jesus (and the God of the Bible) are taken off the path to Hell and go to Heaven, while everyone else goes to Hell. This is my understanding of salvation as told through many scriptures of the Bible, including these noted here.

Here are some more important words from Jesus related to who is going to Heaven versus Hell:

> *Then Jesus said to his disciples, "If any of you wants to be my follower, you must give up your own way, take up your cross, and follow me. If you try to hang on to your life, you will lose it. But if you give up your life for my sake, you will save it. And what do you benefit if you gain the whole world but lose your own soul? <u>Is anything worth more than your soul?</u>"* (Matthew 16:24-26)

Jesus is saying that we need to have a viewpoint from eternity, not just day-to-day. If we want to spend eternity in Heaven with Jesus then we need to listen and follow His words about how to be saved, now!

Furthermore Jesus says:

> *"You can enter God's Kingdom only through the narrow gate. The highway to hell is broad, and its gate is wide for the many who <u>choose</u> that way. But the gateway to life is very narrow and the road is difficult, and only a few ever find it."* (Matthew 7:13-14)

This verse hits the point that many people are not in alignment with God's will through the saving trust in Jesus; however, God is calling all people to listen to these words of the Bible and follow them. God strongly desires that all come to a saving faith in Him. I think the reality is that many people haven't taken the time to truly read the Bible, especially the New Testament, and give it a real shot.

We'll dig into this more in later chapters, but the fact is that we are saved through faith and not by works, so it's not working really hard to be in the "few" as noted above, but it's about having a simple, child-like faith and believing who Jesus is and what He did for us, and being born-again, as discussed above. Let's continue to see what Jesus says to us about saving faith through this example:

> *Then He turned to the woman and said to Simon, "Do you see this woman? I entered your house; you gave Me no water for My feet, but she has washed My feet with her tears and wiped them with the hair of her head. You gave Me no kiss, but this woman has not ceased to kiss My feet since the time I came in. You did not anoint My head with oil, but this woman has anointed My feet with fragrant oil. Therefore I say to you, her sins, which are many, are forgiven, for she loved much. But to whom little is forgiven, the same loves little." Then He said to her, "Your sins are forgiven." And those who sat at the table with Him began to say to themselves, "Who is this who even forgives sins?" Then He said to the woman, "<u>Your faith has saved you</u>. Go in peace."* (Luke 7:44-50 NKJV)

This verse makes it clear that our faith is what saves us (and God's assistance to do so), not our works, even though your works should follow your faith.

Furthermore, Jesus said:

> *Anyone who isn't with me opposes me, and anyone who isn't working with me is actually working against me.* (Matthew 12:30)

This verse reinforces Jesus' other statements (John 14:6, etc.) that He is the only way to the Father and Heaven, not many ways.

Overall, let's clearly remember that all these are the words of Jesus, the one who said He and God are one in the same, and that He said that He's the only way to Heaven. He raised people from the dead and did many other miracles witnessed by thousands of people. He showed love and respect to all people. He was so consistent with His life's actions.

Therefore, we really have just two choices: believe 100% of Jesus' words or don't believe any of His words. We can't pick and choose the things we like or want to accept—it's either all or none. He was the perfect God-man, or He was a great liar. Let's choose the former and really believe and take action on His words above!

4: The Ultimate Dare

Reading words from the Bible, from 2000 years ago, can sometimes open up doubt in our minds. We may wonder, "Are these really the words of Jesus, the Son of God?" There can be so many reasons to doubt, and that is normal. But at the end of the day, <u>we need to believe in something</u>.

We need to have faith in some path of life, one of the options out there. Even if we say we don't believe in anything related to faith or religion, the fact is that we have rejected the things we have heard about religions, so we do actually believe in something—our belief is disagreement with religion. Whether we want to think deeply about it or not, we do put our stake in the ground and say, "I believe 'this' will get me to Heaven." Or maybe it is, "I don't believe in any religion, and I think it will be lights out (consciousness and soul) when I die." Or maybe just, "I don't care!"

No matter what your viewpoint is on life, death, Heaven and Hell, you have to know that you are putting so much at stake on this belief that you have. When we do that, make our decision on "the way we believe," we are putting the largest bet ever that we are correct on "our truth." It is a much, much larger bet than putting $1,000,000 down on the roulette table and hoping for either red or black to come through, knowing it's a 50/50 chance.

Whether you consider yourself a Christian, a Muslim, a Jew, a Hindu, a Buddhist, a Taoist or maybe agnostic, atheist or just generally "spiritual," you are making a bet on eternity relative to what you believe. Stop and think about that. Really, stop and think—are you betting on red or black at the roulette table of eternity? Knowing that if you are wrong you will have dire consequences?

For this part I'm going to ask you to take some action to help you understand the depth of the decision we all are making here on earth during our relatively short lives. This is meant to bring some gravity to our bet on "red or black" on the roulette table of life. This "Ultimate Dare" is designed to give you a profound, albeit brief, glimpse into the stark reality of isolation and the unending nature of eternity, which is central to understanding Hell.

I believe strongly that we all have one shot—this life—to make things right with God and secure our spot in Heaven (referred to as the "Book of Life" in the Bible. See Revelation 20:11-15). The option between Heaven and Hell awaits us all, and once we go to either place it lasts for eternity, and we can't change locations.

THE ULTIMATE DARE

For this ultimate dare you'll need to prepare in the following way:

1. Choose a time when no one will be at your home or everyone is sleeping. The time should be later at night, during darkness and preferably late in the evening. It should be as quiet as possible.

2. Bring a flashlight, digital clock (or your phone, if you have willpower to not use it for anything other than a timer and light!) and a notebook and pen. Leave your water bottle, blanket or anything else behind. Go find the most unlikable place in your home, if possible. The best place would be a basement area that is unfinished, perhaps by a furnace, with concrete floor, no carpet or flooring. The goal is to get away from the comforts we normally seek.

3. Go to that place and turn off all the lights and use your flashlight.

4. Sit on the floor (not a couch, a pillow or anything comfortable). The goal is ultimate vulnerability and isolation.

5. Set up your clock so you can see it and then shut off the flashlight.

6. Sit there for 30 minutes. Ask yourself, "What if I was destined to sit here for eternity?" Ask yourself, "What do I really believe about what happens after I die?" Ask yourself, "Am I 100% confident in what I believe, do I have peace about this decision?" In this position you will not have

any friends, no family, no light, no communication, no fun. But, you have your thought life with you. Don't worry about eating or drinking, that will not be necessary.

7. At the end of 30 minutes consider sitting there another 30 minutes if you're not very deep in thought about your future, after you die. If after 1 hour you still aren't there, continue on.

8. When you feel that you've made progress in considering eternity in these conditions, turn on the flashlight and start writing your feelings in the notebook. What did you think about? What concerned you? What questions did you have? Did you think about how confident you are in your current choice of belief relative to spiritual things, Heaven and Hell? Write down all your relevant thoughts.

9. Now review what you wrote. What did you think about? How does this make you feel? Did your viewpoint change at all? Is the seriousness of your future, after you die, embedded deeper in you and you just need to really stop and think about it more? After this, go ahead and get your things and continue on with life.

10. Consider putting a reminder on your phone to review your notebook once a week or once a month. Relive your time going through this process and keep thinking about what your life means relative to eternity. The speed of day-to-day life will quickly seep back in and it's easy to defer thoughts about a huge decision relative to

THE ULTIMATE DARE

Heaven or Hell. Revisiting your journal will get you back to the importance of really giving time to the most important issue of our lives—where we will spend eternity.

Now, sitting in the dark in an uncomfortable way for 30 or 60 minutes is not anywhere close to the reality of Hell. Jesus said many times that there will be "wailing and gnashing of teeth" in Hell. Also, Satan and the demons will be there, and we know they won't make it pleasant. There will also be many, many other people there in the same horrible condition and you will hear them in their strife—that is where the wailing and gnashing of teeth noises are coming from, of course.

This doesn't stop after 30 or 60 minutes. It never stops. It's so hard to imagine eternity in our minds, going on and on and on and on. Not one day, not two days, not one week, not one month, but years and years and years. And it's almost unfathomable to think we could be sitting there in agony for this long. But that is exactly what the Bible says about Hell. It's up to you if you believe that or not, and up to you if you believe in Jesus' words or not. It is the ultimate and most important decision of your life.

Are you ready to find peace relative to life's ultimate question—what happens to me when I die? Please read on to the next two chapters for final guidance on this.

However, are you still questioning things? If so, the best thing you can do is to read one or more of the gospels and then the book of Acts right after it. Consider reading all of Matthew (or John) and all of Acts over the next few weeks. Take notes and really contemplate the words in these essential books of the Bible. Make time for this, it is so worth it!

5: Decision Time

Now that we've read many of Jesus' words about life and death and decision making, it's time to pull it all together. Jesus loves every human being and wants all of us to go to Heaven, but He requires a step of faith and trust by us (with His help), and then He will guide the rest of our lives as we seek Him.

Let's remember that God is a God of love. He wants everyone to be saved, which is clearly stated in many verses, such as all of the following verses from the New Testament of the Bible:

> *This is good and pleases God our Savior, <u>who wants everyone to be saved</u> and to understand the truth. For, there is <u>one God</u> and one Mediator who can reconcile God and humanity—the man Christ Jesus. He gave his life to purchase freedom for everyone. This is the message God gave to the world at just the right time.* (1 Timothy 2:3-6)

"For this is how God loved the world: He gave his one and only Son, <u>so that everyone</u> who believes in him will not perish but have eternal life. God sent his Son into the world not to judge the world, but to save the world through him." (John 3:16-17)

The Lord isn't really being slow about his promise, as some people think. No, he is being patient for your sake. <u>He does not want anyone</u> to be destroyed, but wants everyone to repent. (2 Peter 3:9)

In the same way, it is not my heavenly Father's will that even one of these little ones should perish. (Matthew 18:14)

Then Jesus said to his disciples, "If any of you wants to be my follower, you must give up your own way, take up your cross, and follow me. If you try to hang on to your life, you will lose it. But if you give up your life for my sake, you will save it. <u>And what do you benefit if you gain the whole world but lose your own soul? Is anything worth more than your soul?</u>" (Matthew 16:24-26)

And the Good News about the Kingdom will be preached throughout the whole world, <u>so that all nations will hear it</u>; and then the end will come. (Matthew 24:14)

From these verses above, it is clear that God's desire is to see all humans come to the saving knowledge of Him through Christ. God gives everyone a chance (including prior to Christ, which is a subject clarified by other writ-

DECISION TIME

ers). God has put a tugging in our heart to follow Him. God loves us more than anyone can really comprehend!

By reading Jesus' words in the previous chapters we now know all of the following facts:

- No person is "good" in and of themselves
- We are all sinners by nature, at birth, and need a savior
- All of Jesus' words are true and we can trust them. He's either the biggest liar ever, or He is who He says He is. We need to really believe in the latter and there is no middle ground.
- Many people will go to Hell for eternity
- Jesus wants all of us to truly turn to Him in faith, fully trusting Him for what He did for us
- The only way we go to Heaven is through Jesus Christ, as stated by His own words
- We can't earn our way to Heaven, it's only by faith. Good works do not get us to Heaven
- No other religions will get us to Heaven, nor does "no faith" (agnostic, atheists, non-religious, etc.)
- Once in Heaven or Hell, after our lives here on earth, our position there will never change

One visual representation of the innate problem we have with us is depicted in sketch "D" on page 73. Once Adam and Eve sinned in the Garden of Eden at the beginning of the human race, there became a chasm between us and God. This chasm, or separation, is due to our sin, and it ultimately ends in going to Hell if we don't do anything about it. We can't earn our way to Heaven by doing good works—that has absolutely no chance at all. Only "cleansed/saved" people go to Heaven, not "good" people. How do we get "cleansed"? Only by the blood, the sacrifice, of Jesus.

When Jesus was crucified on the cross it was for our sins, for the sins of every single person that ever lived. He was the ultimate sacrifice to <u>cover all of our sins</u> and make us white as snow, make us appear sinless to God (cleansed), and give us a ticket to Heaven. You should know that if you were the only person on earth that Jesus would have died just for you!

Image "D," on the opposite page depicts Jesus and the cross bridging the impermeable gap between us and God, and for those who accept and trust Jesus by faith as their savior, we have a path over the chasm and into the hands of the loving God, for eternity. Only Jesus can bridge that gap for us, nothing else!

Jesus told him, "I am the way, the truth, and the life. No one can come to the Father except through me." (John 14:6)

Another way to visualize the difference between focusing on life on earth, which is short and ends in physical death, and a life that is born again and promised eternal life with God in Heaven (vs. eternal life in Hell), is displayed in Image "E" on page 74.

All praise to God, the Father of our Lord Jesus Christ. It is by his great mercy that we have been <u>born again</u>, because God raised Jesus Christ from the dead. Now we live with great expectation, and we have a priceless inheritance—an inheritance

DECISION TIME

JOHN 14:6

WHAT HAPPENS WHEN I DIE?

ETERNITY IN HELL

PHYSICAL BIRTH ⟶ PHYSICAL DEATH

UNSAVED LIFE   NEW LIFE IN CHRIST   ETERNAL LIFE IN HEAVEN

SPIRITUAL BIRTH ⟶ IN GOD'S PRESENCE

1 PETER 1:3-5   (E)

> *that is kept in heaven for you, pure and undefiled, beyond the reach of change and decay. And through your faith, God is protecting you by his power until you receive this salvation, which is ready to be revealed on the last day for all to see.* (1 Peter 1:3-5)

Without Christ we have no hope beyond the grave. With Christ we have a wonderful hope and assurance in a beautiful afterlife to live with Him for eternity. We get to be done with the trials and tribulations of this world. Wow, what an amazing thing to look forward to. We really need to grasp the significance of this!

Let's look at a visual of eternity again to really think about how incredibly important our decisions during our very short life on earth are. Our life is just a short blip in the span of eternity. It seems long to us, but not compared to eternity, the rest of our conscious life. Therefore, it's so important to think about eternity more and more during our everyday life. Don't just go on with life and not think about where you will spend eternity, as your soul, your future life fully depends on this.

With that, let's dive into what Jesus says about a true conversion of an individual, a true belief and trust in Him, a life-changing moment:

> *There was a man named Nicodemus, a Jewish religious leader who was a Pharisee. After dark one evening, he came to speak with Jesus. "Rabbi," he said, "we all know that God has sent you to teach us. Your miraculous signs are evidence that God is with you." Jesus replied, "I tell you the truth, unless you are born again, you cannot see the Kingdom of God."" "What do you mean?" exclaimed Nicodemus. "How*

can an old man go back into his mother's womb and be born again?" Jesus replied, "I assure you, <u>no one can enter the Kingdom of God without</u> being born of water and the Spirit. Humans can reproduce only human life, but the Holy Spirit gives birth to spiritual life. So don't be surprised when I say, "You must be born again." (John 3:1-7)

So what does born again mean? Jesus says, "born of the Spirit" (that is, the Holy Spirit, one of the Trinity: God the Father, God the Son and God the Holy Spirit). See Chapter 3: Section 3.5 (p.54), for discussion on "born of water," as it isn't something you have to actively do.

This process of being born again, or "saved," is not something we muster up solely by ourselves, but an act of faith by us and the assistance of the Holy Spirit. It's not 100% us doing it and not 100% God doing it, but it's a blend of the two.

In essence, **to be "born again" means receiving a new, spiritual life from God through the Holy Spirit**, marked by a heart-level belief and trust in Jesus.

He draws us and we must respond. We must act in full faith and trust. It is realizing that we are truly sinful at birth, that we need our sins covered, and Jesus is the only way to do it—He pays the penalty for our sin. The penalty for human sin must be paid, and one way is by going to Hell and one way is having Jesus pay it for us, period.

Being saved is acknowledging that Jesus is both the Son of God and equal to, and a part of, God. He is part of the Trinity. It is accepting Jesus as our savior and fully trusting Him and believing who He is and what He did for us.

DECISION TIME

It includes turning from (repenting of) our old ways of life, which is a process that really truly starts at the onset of the born-again/conversion/saved experience. Then it is followed by living a life led by the Holy Spirit, not perfect, but aiming in the right direction. This conversion process is just the beginning of a new life and we will talk about the next steps extensively below and in the next chapter.

This is a heart decision we need to make.

Jesus uses the following as one analogy to help us understand this step:

> *When Jesus saw what was happening, he was angry with his disciples. He said to them, "Let the children come to me. Don't stop them! For the Kingdom of God belongs to those who are like these children. I tell you the truth, anyone who doesn't receive the Kingdom of God like a child will never enter it.' Then he took the children in his arms and placed his hands on their heads and blessed them."* (Mark 10:14-16)

This analogy reinforces that we need to drop our pretenses, drop our excuses, look at the overwhelming evidence, and accept Jesus for who He said He is and what He can do for us! Just like young children believe their (honest) parents, with humble dependance, because they trust them, we must believe in Jesus this way.

How do you get saved? It is by trusting and believing that Jesus took all the penalty of our sin. It's by confessing your sins and believing in His saving gift of eternal life with Him, that He died for all our sins and will cover them. It is truly giving your heart, mind and soul to Jesus. It is trusting and following Jesus, period!

It is often stressed that people should pray a prayer of salvation to truly be saved. Well, the prayer is not what gets you into Heaven—it's your heart. Nowhere in the scriptures did Jesus or the disciples give an example of telling people to pray a specific prayer for salvation. Instead, you simply get saved by trusting (truly believing) that Jesus died for your sins. Jesus often said to people "follow me." That's what we need to do!

This trusting turns into a close personal relationship with God if it is truly heartfelt. You don't pray a prayer and then forget about Jesus for the rest of your life—that is not getting saved, that is not being born again. If your heart has really turned over to Jesus, fully trusting in what He has done for us, then you are saved, born-again, and your name is written in the "Book of Life" and you will spend eternity with God and Jesus.

Now, is it bad to pray a prayer that helps you cement your trust in Jesus? No. But the prayer alone without true trust does nothing.

One common form of a prayer that can accompany your trust in Jesus is something like the following:

> Jesus, take me as I am—I'm a sinner and can't do this myself—I believe that you are the true Son of God, that you died for all my sins, to cover them for me, and that you are the only way to salvation—I ask you in my heart to be my Lord and Savior—and I renounce my old ways, turn away from them, turn towards you with my new

life, and ask you for forgiveness of all my sins. Please take me into your hands and guide the rest of my life along your path.

Again, this prayer alone, without true trust, faith and belief in who Jesus is and what He did for us, does nothing. It's not a "magic prayer." However, once you put your true faith in Jesus as your savior you now have the winning ticket!

Your whole life is going to change because Jesus has you now—you will be guided by God, through the help of the Holy Spirit, to start a new path for life. This is not just believing that this can be done; this is true freedom. It may not feel different right away, but it is, and you will see!

Jesus died for us and He will wipe 100% of our sins away (past, current, future) through a true heart conversion. Only Jesus really knows each person's heart and what they have done with this decision. I don't know who is truly saved and pastors don't know who is truly saved—only God does.

Just to clear things up with some jargon or word descriptions, I want to point out that all of these word choices mean the same thing relative to one's position with Jesus, the God of the universe:

- Saved
- True conversion
- Born again
- True Christian (which, should be just "Christian," but I believe there are a lot of unsaved peo-

ple who wear the Christian title)
- Saving faith
- Secured eternity In Heaven (name written in the Lamb's Book of Life)

I list these as it can be confusing and people use different words for different things, but within the context of everything said in this book, these are all equal or the same.

Now, the Bible talks about fruit of the Spirit, which are essentially Godly attributes lived out in people. These are the best way to have a good idea if someone is saved, over the long run after conversion, not on day one! We will talk about these fruit of the Spirit more in the next chapter.

Many people may feel that "signing up to follow Jesus" is just a long list of rules, things we shouldn't do, and that this way must be very boring. However, it's actually the total opposite—it's true freedom from the things in this life that pull us down and tear us apart.

God is love and freedom, not an overseer of a prison or a mean teacher or boss. You don't really feel that true freedom until you take a step of faith towards Him, as described above. Jesus offers true joy for us, in ways we have not felt before.

Here is one commonly used analogy relative to understanding what the Bible calls "believing in Jesus." This analogy drives home the difference between "head knowledge" and "heart knowledge/trust". Let's say that you are in an airplane and the engines fail and the plane is starting to take a nose-dive towards earth. You were told before takeoff that there is a parachute under your seat. Now, you can believe that the parachute under your seat can save you and not put it on. But, of course, just believing it does not save you. You need to reach down and actually put on that parachute, then it will save you.

It is the same with Jesus—you can't just have head knowledge that He saves (believing the parachute below you but not putting it on), but you need to take action with your heart and really move towards Jesus in faith and trust, as described in this chapter (which is actually putting on the parachute).

Similar to this analogy, the Bible tells us that even demons and Satan believe in Jesus (head knowledge), but they obviously don't have freedom and salvation in Jesus because they lack a heart decision, trust and faith in what He has done.

Let's look at this important verse that divides "believing" in Jesus versus 'trusting Jesus as your savior':

> *You say you have faith, for you believe that there is one God. Good for you! <u>Even the demons believe this</u>, and they tremble in terror.* (James 2:19)

So don't stop and say "I already believe Jesus," if you are not trusting in Him to be your savior—that is false hope. We must go deeper than head knowledge!

Here is a second analogy for true faith in Christ. While no analogy is perfect when we are trying to describe true trust in Jesus Christ, the following widely used analogy is a good one:

The great tightrope walker Blondin strung a wire from one side of the Niagara Falls to the other. A crowd gathered to watch him attempt to walk out over the deadly falls. The silent tension turned to cheers as they watched him walk out, turn and come back. He asked the crowd, "How many believe that I can walk to the other side and back while pushing a wheelbarrow?" To which they shouted, "We believe, we believe!" And, Blondin did in fact walk out and back with a wheelbarrow. Upon his return, Blondin asked, "Who believes I could push a man in this wheelbarrow while walking out and back on the wire?" Again the crowd responded with enthusiastic affirmation. "OK," he asked, "Who would like to get in?" The crowd fell silent. Trusting Christ is not simply assenting to the facts of the gospel message, there is a decision that implies actually getting into the wheelbarrow.[3]

True believing, trusting and following Christ is somewhat similar to me or you getting in a wheelbarrow that is pushed across the tightrope between Hell and Heaven by Jesus Christ. Your essential action needs to be to get in the wheelbarrow and trust Jesus, as you can never get across on that tightrope (to Heaven) on your own. We need to go from head knowledge to heart trusting.

Do we need to start getting our life cleaned up, give up addicting things, and be 'better' <u>before</u> we approach Jesus in faith, asking Him to save us? Absolutely not! Jesus wants us to come as we are, accept and trust Him as our

---

3   From "The Compass", https://www.cru.org/us/en/train-and-grow/bible-studies/compass.html

DECISION TIME

savior, then He'll help us work through the dirt and issues of our life. In fact, Jesus made a point of this by saying that He came to heal the sick, not the well. Which, He meant, He came for people that realize that they are in need of a savior, not those who think they are just fine as is, without Jesus:

> *Later, Matthew invited Jesus and his disciples to his home as dinner guests, along with many tax collectors and other disreputable sinners. But when the Pharisees saw this, they asked his disciples, "Why does your teacher eat with such scum?" When Jesus heard this, he said, "Healthy people don't need a doctor—sick people do."* (Matthew 9:10-12)

Does being saved/born-again save us from all of our sins in the past, present and future? Yes, it does! There are three tenses of this freedom:

1. "You have been set free from the penalty of sin"

2. "You are being set free from the power of sin"

3. "You will be set free from the presence of sin" (in Heaven)[4]

Wow, that is remarkable! We are wiped totally clean and Jesus will hold us close so that we are looked at as clean when we die and go to the judgment seat of God.

But how are we going to change? Many of us feel like we have already tried in many ways. Also, many of us feel that there was no reason to change before our eyes were opened by the Holy Spirit through our conversion.

---

4   https://www.bible.com/reading-plans/53242-bioy-25classic/day/257 *(added words in parentheses)*

We are not left alone once converted/saved, but we now have the power of the Holy Spirit with us and guiding us. The fact is, as I can attest to, most of the time you don't need to muster up the energy to change, but you actually start feeling subtly (or severely) convicted of things that are not pleasing to God, and you just want to start to change based on that (and your new found love for God!). You start wanting to please God as you get to know Him more.

Furthermore, when we have truly given our hearts to God through Jesus in this way, God promises that He'll never leave us or forsake us—we will never be on our own again:

> *So be strong and courageous! Do not be afraid and do not panic before them. For the Lord your God will personally go ahead of you. <u>He will neither fail you nor abandon you</u>.* (Deuteronomy 31:6)

From the New Testament this is reinforced with this verse:

> *Don't love money; be satisfied with what you have. For God has said, "<u>I will never fail you. I will never abandon you.</u>"* (Hebrews 13:5)

How comforting is that? Never alone again! In fact, our whole world changes when we accept Jesus as our savior. I'm not saying that things are easy or perfect when you get saved—they are not—but they are different in a good way. We now have something permanent to hold onto!

Getting saved is critical and essential step number one. After that we will start to find how to live in His, Jesus' strength (not ours). God and Jesus promise the strength of the Holy Spirit for us to rely on to do our best to live out what God calls us to:

> *Then he said to me, "This is what the Lord says to Zerubbabel: It is not by force nor by strength, <u>but by my Spirit, says the Lord of Heaven's Armies</u>."* (Zechariah 4:6)

Furthermore, God talks about the other ways He is with us in our new journey:

> *Three different times I begged the Lord to take it away. Each time he said, "My grace is all you need. My power works best in weakness." So now I am glad to boast about my weaknesses, so that the power of Christ can work through me.* (2 Corinthians 12:8-9)

> *But you belong to God, my dear children. You have already won a victory over those people, <u>because the Spirit who lives in you is greater than the spirit who lives in the world</u>.* (1 John 4:4)

Wow, what a relief! We don't need to muscle through life on our own. We don't have to call ourselves a failure. We have strength given to us way beyond our own, through the Holy Spirit. We'll never be perfect, but we'll be forgiven and given His grace. We'll also have the Holy Spirit in us to convict us of our sins so that we continue to repent and run from sin, not live in them and say that they are okay.

Are you ready to give your life to God through a personal relationship with Jesus? Are you ready to truly trust Jesus? If you are, praise the Lord! The only real step you need to do first is to truly trust in your heart who Jesus is and what He did for you, period!

After that, there are several other important and practical steps that you should set in motion. You can start by taking time in prayer with God. You can pray the words in the example faith prayer earlier in this section. You can start reading the Gospels (Matthew, Mark, Luke, John), and the book of Acts.

After that, surround yourself with other born-again Christians that have been on this path longer so that they can help you move forward in the faith. It's also so critical to tell another Christian what you have done!

Joining a Bible-centered, Jesus-focused church with true teachings is absolutely vital to your journey. We are built to be in community, not alone! Engaging in that church, including small connect groups, and with other believers outside of church to strengthen and encourage each other along the way is essential. We can't do this alone on Earth. God makes it clear that we need each other.

Reading the Bible yourself (or listening to an audio version) is also a fundamental need of all people following Jesus. Hearing the word of God at church is great, but we absolutely need to read it ourselves. This is the best way that Jesus/God speaks to us, through His written word. We are called to read, listen, and meditate on His word, as it will continue to transform and strengthen us. There are some great Bible Apps out there that will help us do this, in addition to having an old-fashioned (and wonderful!) paper Bible! There are a lot of Bible translations available, but consider the New Living Translation (NLT) or New International Version (NIV) for your Bible.

DECISION TIME

Here are four great resources for newly saved people: the first two are Bible Apps to listen to God (written and audio), the third is a free printed Bible and an option to speak with someone about your faith, and the fourth is a wonderful Instagram channel of a wise young man speaking the simple truths about Jesus and the Bible:

1. **YouVersion Bible App.** It contains all parts/books of the Bible in reading and listening formats, in many Bible translations. It also has great daily podcast-like videos of the scripture of the day, only 2 to 3 minutes long.

2. **The audio Bible App with Nicky and Pippa Gumbel** (feel free to focus on the New Testament at first). This gives very short sermons and explanations for the daily readings, plus the reading of the Bible text itself:

3. **Free New Testament Bible:** www.harvest.org/bible (1-800-821-3300). You can also use this number to talk to someone about trusting Jesus as your savior and/or praying for you. Greg Laurie is the general editor of this New Testament. Greg also has a great Instagram channel under his name.

4. **Instagram Channel with great short videos (needgod.net7).** This evangelist, Ryan Hemelaar, has great videos of him taking tough questions from others or diving deeper into critical questions of Christianity and the Bible.

Another excellent thing to do before or after trusting Christ as your savior is to join a small group at a Bible-believing church that is for new believers and those who want to know more and ask questions about Christ. Christ describes His followers as the "Body of Christ," and He wants us to be in regular real-time communication with others to strengthen each other.

One of the best groups for people considering, seeking or newly trusting Christ is called Alpha, and it is offered at churches throughout the world. You can find more information about Alpha here (www.alpha.org, www.alphausa.org, and search "Alpha Course" on Wikipedia). This is a great first step if you still aren't quite there with what you are reading in this book about Jesus, a safe and casual place to ask questions and consider Jesus more.

Are you still wanting more answers to this whole topic of Biblical authority, that there is only one way, understanding more on being converted/saved, and many more questions about the Bible? One excellent resource for answering a ton of practical questions we all have, or have had, are the books and videos by Cliffe Knechtle. He is a pastor, but is probably more broadly known for his efforts going around to college campuses throughout the US and having hundreds of compassionate, yet direct, dialogues with ad hoc groups of students who join him in open-air discussions.

Cliffe Knechtle has also written books that catalog the most common questions he gets, and has great video clips of these college "debates" and other venues for him answering life's tough questions. Give him a try at: https://givemeananswer.org/ or on Instagram at ask_cliffe or cliff.knechtle.

What does a changed life look like? Chapter 6 is devoted to this topic, but let's first take a brief look at what a close relationship looks like between two people as a comparison. For close relationships between humans, there are at least three essential parts:

> **Communication**: When you have a close committed relationship with someone, say a good marriage or close friend, you are in regular communication because you desire it. Same with God—when you're in love with your maker, you desire to be with Him very often through prayer, worship and Bible reading/listening.

> **Trust**: We trust our loved ones yet sometimes they still let us down (and we let them down). We need to trust Christ with our whole being, as He will never let us down. He said He is our "strength and shield," He says He'll always be with us, and He promises us eternity with Him.

Actions that show love: You have to walk-the-talk in a relationship with a person that you love, right? In the same way, we need to walk out your faith in persistence in trying to be obedient to God. Can we be perfect? No, but we are called to seek holiness: *"You must be holy because I (God) am holy."* (1 Peter 1:16) We are called to seek God first and try our best and He'll be there every step of the way to assist us in this new journey.

Jesus loves us and desires the most intimate and real relationship with us that is possible between a human and God. He desires it to be much closer than any relationship we can have with people on earth.

None of this happens instantly—in fact, this goal of an extremely intimate relationship with God/Jesus is a lifelong pursuit. This relationship is just the beginning of an eternal relationship with God; it prepares us for Heaven with our creator, something to really look forward to!

> *Yet God has made everything beautiful for its own time. He has planted eternity in the human heart, but even so, people cannot see the whole scope of God's work from beginning to end.* (Ecclesiastes 3:11)

6: Followers -- What's Next?

Getting into Heaven is essential step number one, and how to get into Heaven is discussed in prior chapters. We can never earn our way into Heaven by doing good works. I want to emphasize this—getting into Heaven by being saved is only through the gift God gave us, Jesus, and His grace—we can never "earn" our way to Heaven, never! This chapter is the opposite of earning our way to Heaven. It is what God desires for our hearts to be like once we have already come to faith and trusted Him to be our Lord and Savior.

Doing the things below without being born-again doesn't get you into Heaven. But God calls all saved people to turn from their old ways and steadily turn more and more to the ways God calls us to be. True faith in Jesus naturally expresses itself by a changed life. God wants saved Christians to be oriented fundamentally different than prior to our born-again/saved experience, and I hope to share the highlights of what Jesus said about this in this chapter.

Here are two important scriptures that tell us that true conversion results in changes in our lives that align with God's attributes, and God wants these attributes to become more evident as time goes on in our relationship with Him:

> *"You can identify them by their fruit, that is, <u>by the way they act</u>. Can you pick grapes from thornbushes, or figs from thistles? A good tree produces good fruit, and a bad tree produces bad fruit."* (Matthew 7:16-17)

> *But the Holy Spirit produces this kind of fruit in our lives: love, joy, peace, patience, kindness, goodness, faithfulness, gentleness, and self-control. There is no law against these things!* (Galatians 5:22-23)

What a wonderful list of attributes. These are hard or impossible to do on our own, but we have a great shot at all of them with the help of God's Holy Spirit!

Furthermore, believe it or not, what we do with our lives here on earth after being saved will affect both those around us here on earth and also what type of position we have in Heaven. Yes, our obedience to God following being saved has a double blessing!

The Bible guides Jesus' followers to do many things that essentially help us get aligned with how Jesus acted while here on earth.

FOLLOWERS -- WHAT'S NEXT?

The following actions and efforts can be considered the essential ingredients of what Jesus is looking for in those who have trusted Him as their savior:

1. Read His Word, the Bible
2. Strive to put God #1 in all parts of our lives
3. Continue to repent and turn from any repeated sinful behavior
4. Pray regularly
5. Love all people
6. Belong to and engage with a church community that is focused on doing these things (you can't do this alone)
7. Share this gospel message with others
8. Give to the church, the poor and widows

These items above and the discussion on each below are really just a quick overview and introduction to a well-rounded and effective relationship with Christ. These things rarely take place overnight or really fast—it's a process—but the point is that these are essential to dig into over the coming days, weeks, months, and years.

God wants us to put Him first in our life, before all other things, which is really, really hard, and doesn't come naturally. That means, before our family, before our spouse, before our job, before our entertainment. Of course, God wants us to carefully prioritize and give our best to these other important things, but He calls us to put Him first. These items help us start walking the path of fulfilling these essential items as a follower of Christ.

1) Read His Word, the Bible

"But Jesus told him, 'No! The Scriptures say, "People do not live by bread alone, but by every word that comes from the mouth of God."'" (Matthew 4:4)

Here we see that it is vitally critical that we all read and do our best to live by the Bible. The Bible is the primary way God speaks to us. He calls us to read it, replay it in our head (meditate on it), memorize it so we have it later in our mind to pull out for our help and strength in times of need, and do our best to live it out (with the help and strength of the Holy Spirit). This is the best way we listen to God, by reading and meditating on His Word.

I recommend that you start out by reading all four gospels (Matthew, Mark, Luke and John) if you haven't yet. Then read Acts right after. These books of the Bible lay the foundational truths of when Jesus was on earth and they will bring all of Jesus' words here into context.

Beyond that I recommend that you read the rest of the New Testament, the Psalms and Proverbs, then the Old Testament, starting at Genesis. I can tell you that I personally still find a lot of the Old Testament challenging to fully comprehend, but it has essential truths for us throughout it. The Bible App noted in Chapter 5 (by Nicky and Pippa Gumbel) is a great alternative to reading the Bible yourself.

FOLLOWERS -- WHAT'S NEXT?

2) Strive to put God #1 in all parts of our lives

"Get out of here, Satan," Jesus told him. "For the Scriptures say, 'You must worship the Lord your God and serve only him.'" (Matthew 4:10)

God makes it clear that we are only to love one God, Him, and that we are to put Him first in our lives. This is Jesus requoting the first of the 10 Commandments of the Old Testament before He came to earth (Exodus 20:3). Throughout the Bible, God tells us that He is a jealous God and won't stand for people worshiping other gods (other false gods, as there is only one true God, Jesus). While very few people that call themselves Christians literally bow down to a different god, it's relatively easy to put other things first in our lives and be more devoted to other things before God and put God down the list.

God is challenging us to truly put Him first in this and other scriptures of the Bible. What are other things that we humans often worship (put number one in our lives)? Money? Our jobs? Our spouse/partner, free time, other false gods, sinful things, vacations, partying? Our phones? God calls us to think about what is currently first in our hearts and get things in alignment with really putting Him first.

Jesus replied, "<u>You must love the Lord your God with all your heart, all your soul, and all your mind. This is the first and greatest commandment.</u> A second is equally important: Love your neighbor as yourself. The entire law and all the demands of the prophets are based on these two commandments."
(Matthew 22:37-40)

WHAT HAPPENS WHEN I DIE?

Let's take a minute to think about the "first and greatest commandment" relative to other relationships we have. If you love your spouse (or parent or child or friend or significant other) "with all your heart," then how do you treat them? Do you ignore them? Don't talk to them? Don't visit them? And when you do spend time with them, is it a burden? Do you want to spend a few minutes and then "get on with other things"? Do you intentionally do things that anger them on a regular basis, or just not think about what they care about? Do you lie to them regularly?...of course you don't!

If you truly love someone then you treat them the best you can, the way you would want to be treated. You make time for them, you put them first, you are straight-up with them and you look forward to spending more time with them so you can get to know them better. In general, this is how you start putting God first in your life!

Furthermore, we have consequences to our actions relative to putting God first:

"Anyone who listens to my teaching and follows it is wise, like a person who builds a house on solid rock. Though the rain comes in torrents and the floodwaters rise and the winds beat against that house, it won't collapse because it is built on bedrock. <u>But anyone who hears my teaching and doesn't obey it is foolish</u>, like a person who builds a house on sand. When the rains and floods come and the winds beat against that house, it will collapse with a mighty crash." (Matthew 7:24-27)

These verses all focus on putting Jesus/God first, to do "His will." That is the perpetual goal of the saved Christian, a daily and lifelong pursuit.

3) Continue to repent and turn from any repeated sinful behavior

"From then on Jesus began to preach, 'Repent of your sins and turn to God, for the Kingdom of Heaven is near.'" (Matthew 4:17)

What do we need to repent of? Well, we are all sinners by definition, innately (Romans 3:23), so we need to turn from our ways and turn towards God's ways. This world we live in will continually provide temptation on a daily basis and God calls us to fight against that, using His strength.

When we do fall, which we will, God calls us to immediately come to Him, ask for forgiveness and repent against that sin. And then do it over and over and over again when we fall. It's similar to when we do something wrong to our spouse or loved ones, it's best to ask them for forgiveness and have a fresh start.

In addition to the 10 commandments that are first listed in the Old Testament, Jesus and other New Testament writers make it clear that the original commandments still hold true and they elaborate more on what is sin.

Jesus makes it clear that repentance is something you don't wait around for—we need to do it when we come to the Lord for the first time being born-again, and then we need to continue to do it when we fall to sin. Note that this process of regular repentance is not trying to make sure we erase every sin along the way, as Jesus has already done that when we got saved. At the time of being saved our previous sins and all future sins are covered over by the blood He shed for our atonement on the cross.

However, confessing and turning away from our sins is needed so that we are actively trying to keep those sins out of our lives and that we are obedient to Christ by doing it. Furthermore, it lifts off the cloud of shame that we often have after sinning, and God does not want us living in shame—He wants us living in freedom and joy!

4) Pray regularly

In human relationships we talk to each other regularly (speak and listen) and we spend time with each other to get closer. Similarly, with God, we talk to Him by praying and we listen to Him primarily through reading the Bible (of course, through church and with other Christians are other ways we have communication/communion with God).

Even though God knows all of our thoughts already, He still wants us to pray regularly, as it is building our relationship with Him, and He loves to hear from us each time we speak! It is the most powerful tool He gave us to ask Him to help us and others go through life with Him closer to us, including answered prayers.

The ultimate goal is to pray every day, hopefully including multiple small chats with God throughout the day! The best time to pray is first thing in the morning without other distractions (and even better when it's before we look at our phones!), and before we get tired out from all the things that happened in that day. This is part of putting God first in all things. Listen to what Jesus says about prayer:

"When you pray, don't be like the hypocrites who love to pray publicly on street corners and in the synagogues where everyone can see them. I tell you the truth, that is all the reward they will ever get. But when you pray, go away by yourself, shut the door behind you, and pray to your Father in private. Then your Father, who sees everything, will reward you. When you pray, don't babble on and on as the Gentiles do. They think their prayers are answered merely by repeating their words again and again. Don't be like them, for your Father knows exactly what you need even before you ask him! Pray like this: Our Father in heaven, may your name be kept holy. May your Kingdom come soon. May your will be done on earth, as it is in heaven. Give us today the food we need, and forgive us our sins, as we have forgiven those who sin against us. And don't let us yield to temptation, but rescue us from the evil one."
(Matthew 6:5-13)

This is the model for our praying. While it doesn't have to go "on and on" for an hour or two or more, it should be regular (daily and sporadically throughout is extremely rewarding!) and should be specific. Now, there are whole books dedicated to discussing prayer life with Jesus, so this will not be all encompassing.

But a few key points about prayer:

a. Prayer should align with God's word, the Bible.

b. Not all prayers are answered the way we want. God knows what is best for us in the long run and He allows things for reasons we can't understand, but we need to trust Him.

c. Expect that God will hear every prayer, but also know that there are essentially three ways God will respond—with a "yes," a "no," or a "wait." God is God alone and He knows best!

d. We should keep asking for things we feel are in alignment with the Bible and we don't see action on. This is what we are supposed to do in faith.

5) Love all people

Jesus is love and He calls us to share that love with others. In fact, He goes as far as to say "love your enemies." Wow, that isn't easy. But as we get to know God better and we come to realize more the depth of what He did for us when He died on the cross for our sins, we come to understand that we need to love others with a pure love.

When we do this, we are fulfilling His commands to us and it does so many wonderful things for both us and the ones we are showing love. Here are two of the many verses in the Bible that talk about this:

Jesus replied, "'You must love the Lord your God with all your heart, all your soul, and all your mind.' This is the first and greatest commandment.

A second is equally important: 'Love your neighbor as yourself.' The entire law and all the demands of the prophets are based on these two commandments." (Matthew 22:37-40)

"Then these righteous ones will reply, 'Lord, when did we ever see you hungry and feed you? Or thirsty and give you something to drink? Or a stranger and show you hospitality? Or naked and give you clothing? When did we ever see you sick or in prison and visit you?' And the King will say, 'I tell you the truth, when you did it to one of the least of these my brothers and sisters, you were doing it to me!'" (Matthew 25:37-40)

Loving people like we love ourselves isn't easy, but it is what God calls us to. As we continue to develop our relationship with God this gets easier and easier!

6) Belong to and engage with a church community that is focused on doing these things (you can't do this alone)

Our relationship with Christ is a vertical one, but God has made it clear that we also must focus on gathering together as Christians to build each other up as a team, not a solo sport (our horizontal relationships). While going to church regularly is vitally important for corporate worship, hearing God speak through your pastor and bonding with other Christians, it really can't be the only thing we do to really strive in our role as a follower of Christ.

To grow the way God wants us to we need to come together in our homes and talk and pray with our family and friends. We also should engage in formal Bible studies, hang out and have fun with other Christians, and have 1 or 2 very trusted close Christian friends that we can be accountable with and share our deepest challenges.

Putting these things together along with the key vertical relationship items discussed above (prayer, Bible reading) are guaranteed to help us grow deeper with Christ and help us be more effective battling sin and also doing the works of God's Kingdom here on earth through helping other people. Here is one of the verses from the Bible that discusses this:

Let us think of ways to motivate one another to acts of love and good works. And let us not neglect our meeting together, as some people do, but encourage one another, especially now that the day of his return is drawing near. (Hebrews 10:24-25)

Furthermore, Jesus said the following about coming together:

"I also tell you this: If two of you agree here on earth concerning anything you ask, my Father in heaven will do it for you. For where two or three gather together as my followers, I am there among them." (Matthew 18:19-20)

Now, one caveat with the above, the things asked here need to be in alignment with God's will, and God still gets to decide. But the main message is—trying to walk as a solo follower of Christ doesn't work well at all, we need the strength and community of others!

7) Share this gospel message with others

If you won a million dollars through some type of raffle or contest, and you have a loving spouse and children, would you share this huge blessing of cash with them? Of course you would! In the same way, now that we have found the most important thing in the world, a saving relationship with the one and only God of the world, wouldn't it make sense to share this with your family, friends, co-workers, neighbors, and others? Of course it would!

Part of the reason to believe all the words of the Bible is because of what it has proven already through the 2000 years since Jesus left this earth. Between the time when Jesus rose from the grave and when He ascended to Heaven was 40 days. Within those 40 days He saw hundreds of people, even 500+ at one time.

Of course, these included the original apostles and those closest to Him, but it also included many others not in a close relationship with Him. This relatively small remnant, plus those who believed without seeing Him after He rose, had such a fervent belief in what He said that they started telling everyone about Jesus.

They told their neighbors, total strangers, family, etc. They traveled to different countries to share the good news of the one and only true God. Their actions are so encouraging to see. In fact, a number of them held on to their beliefs to the point of death, when others told them to disavow their God or die.

This small remnant of faithful followers after Christ's resurrection, located in one small country in the Middle East, has now turned into somewhere between 1 and 2.5 billion people (alive today, plus many more who have passed on) who are spread across the entire earth.

Isn't that growth and geographic spread amazing? Through the strength of the Holy Spirit, saved Christians are motivated to share the gospel with others. They share it because it is so personally meaningful and because of their confidence that it is the only way to get saved.

In fact, the great majority of people who have come to a saving faith in Christ started really getting interested in Christ by a 1-on-1 sharing from someone else, not from going to a church or listening to a televangelist on TV. That is the most prominent way that the way of saving faith is shared.

Likewise, God calls all saved/born-again followers to do the same thing, to go share this wonderful news:

Jesus came and told his disciples, "I have been given all authority in heaven and on earth. Therefore, go and make disciples of all the nations, baptizing them in the name of the Father and the Son and the Holy Spirit. Teach these new disciples to obey all the commands I have given you. And be sure of this: I am with you always, even to the end of the age." (Matthew 28:18-20)

As we grow in our relationship with Christ this should come easier, but we know that this is an essential command from the Lord and the last thing He said before He ascended to Heaven, which emphasizes the importance of it. So go share this great news!

8) Give to the church, the poor and widows

Now this discussion is often one that people want to run from or ignore, to be honest. We all work hard for our money and it's not innate to just give it away. However, in both the Old Testament and in the New Testament, God makes it clear that He asks us to give to Him, through our local church, to the poor and needy, and to other godly callings.

The Bible talks about tithing and God encourages us to give offerings beyond this. These acts of faith show that we are putting God first and honoring Him with His requests. Through this, God promises to take care of us in both financial and non-financial ways.

There are four main reasons to give back money and our time to God. First, it's about truly putting God first, then the next is to free ourselves from slavery to money (so it is not first on our list, before God), the third is to help others less fortunate, and the fourth is to help the church and others spread the Word of God (these are not in order of importance).

Here is where Jesus talks about the reason for protecting our hearts:

"No one can serve two masters. For you will hate one and love the other; you will be devoted to one and despise the other. <u>You cannot serve God and be enslaved to money</u>." (Matthew 6:24)

Furthermore, God clearly tells us (and our church) to take care of the poor and widows in these verses:

Pure and genuine religion in the sight of God the Father means caring for orphans and widows in their distress and refusing to let the world corrupt you. (James 1:27)

"Whoever is kind to the poor lends to the Lord, and he will reward them for what they have done." (Proverbs 19:17 NIV)

And God speaks to us through this verse to show the positive outcomes of our giving:

Remember this: Whoever sows sparingly will also reap sparingly, and whoever sows generously will also reap generously. Each of you should give what you have decided in your heart to give, not reluctantly or under compulsion, for God loves a cheerful giver. And God is able to bless you abundantly, so that in all things at all times, having all that you need, you will abound in every good work. (2 Corinthians 9:6-8 NIV)

Let's all consider these and other verses about giving back to God. It's hard, but He calls us to it and there are rewards for doing it!

Now, when we read all the things above it may seem daunting, and in a way it is. However, this is our calling, it is by no means required day one, and not required to be great in all these things. And, again, this is not how we get into Heaven! It's our calling after we are saved.

FOLLOWERS -- WHAT'S NEXT?

No one except Jesus Christ has ever been perfect with all of these commandments and these ways that God wants us to be, as listed above. Nope, not close. We all sin and fall short of His glory and we have a sinful nature from birth. However, there is a huge difference between trying your best, with the help and strength of the Holy Spirit, to follow these, compared to not caring or even knowing about these words from Jesus.

With this, I encourage you to dig into God's Word daily and strive to make Him number one in all parts of your life, as I strive to do the same!

7: Final Thoughts

Life is a beautiful gift, in and of itself. There are so many things to be thankful for in the "here and now." But all of our lives will come to an end someday, often faster than we thought, and sometimes suddenly without warning.

Are you prepared for what happens when you die? Are you 100% confident in your viewpoint on what gives you comfort about the afterlife? Do the words of this book, in particular the words right from the mouth of Jesus, cause you concern at all? Are you questioning your worldview of the afterlife? Are you sure that "being a good person," in and of itself, will take care of you in the afterlife?

I challenge you to do this, at a minimum, if you have any doubts at all. I challenge you to read just two books of the Bible: Matthew and Acts. They are both in the New Testament. They take you from the birth of Jesus to the death of Jesus, His resurrection, His 40 days on earth interacting with people after His resurrection, then the start of the Christian church in Acts. It will not take long to read these two books of the Bible. Think about all the time you spend on your phone or at work, or both! Make this a priority to read these two books. You can swap out Matthew with any of the other gospels (Mark, Luke or John) if you want!

Read it for yourself. Don't take my words here—read it from the source document. I recommend you choose either the NLT (New Living Translation) or NIV (New International Version), but there are other good translations as well.

Then after you have read Matthew and Acts (and feel free to add Mark, Luke and John!), then go back and read Chapters 5 and 6 of this book.

I pray that you find the love and joy of Christ, and that you have great security in your afterlife!

Appendix -- My Story

My life story is not really remarkable at all. I'm sharing this part just for context and I suspect that a number of people can relate to the "normal" or "average" life that I have lived. I'm not a pastor and I don't have a theology degree—I'm just an "average Joe."

I grew up in the suburbs of Minneapolis, Minnesota, about 30 minutes north of downtown Minneapolis (mostly in Coon Rapids). I have two sisters, two half-brothers, and my parents were married until I was 18 years old, then divorced. We lived a "normal" middle-income suburban life, hanging out with friends in our neighborhood all the time and playing in sports that we were interested in.

My dad taught me how to downhill ski and to golf at a young age, and I continue to enjoy both periodically now. I'm thankful for those life-long sporting skills he taught me! He also showed me how to skate and play hockey (and was my coach a couple years), and I loved hockey more than any other sport. I played other sports as well, but overall, I was very average and did it just to keep busy and be around friends.

My mom was the most kind and most fun mom ever. She made it very enjoyable for others to come to our house to live out our youth. She did pretty much everything around the house and made life easy. She even made my bed regularly (yes, I was a slacker in some areas!). School was relatively enjoyable, mostly because of friends, and I found that I could do well at any class subject if I just put my mind to it and worked hard.

Religion and spirituality were not that important in our household nor with my friends, from what I could see. I guess it's common to hang out with people like yourself. We went to church maybe a handful of times each year, for sure on Christmas and Easter. I was put in my Catholic classes (CCD) from elementary through high school. I went to first communion around 1st grade and eventually went through "confirmation" around 11th grade.

While I did do my homework in those CCD classes, memorize some prayers and attend the classes associated with confirmation, as well as attend church periodically, I never had a significant or deep spiritual life. I never took time to pray on my own or with my family members (or anyone). I never read the Bible on my own outside of finishing an assignment for confirmation class.

I recall that when I had my first communion that my godparents gave me a nice new (and big, wow!) Bible and

APPENDIX -- MY STORY

also a soccer ball. They said, "You can use the soccer ball after you are done reading the Bible." If that was the case, I would not have ever used that soccer ball! I don't think I read that Bible at all.

In general, I'd say I just didn't care much about spiritual things and faith. If I ever saw people really into their faith it seemed like it would be boring and they seemed a bit weird. How could they be getting so happy off of "that stuff"? I guess I just felt OK with how I was and didn't feel the need to do anything else.

Looking back now, I do recall one or two occasions that one of our "weird" neighbors invited us to a gathering at their home, which I'm quite certain now that they were describing a truly Christ-following relationship and saving faith to us. But at that time it just went right over my head and I wasn't drawn to it at that time.

At that time I never deeply contemplated the questions in this book: *What Happens When I Die?* and "What's the most important question in life?" I prayed the prayers required at my CCD class and sometimes in church, but it really didn't mean anything (or much) to me. It was basically memorization and rote prayers, not personally impactful. I never really felt the weight of sin, other than feeling a bit bad when I knew I did something relatively extreme, which I did do sometimes.

My personality was more of a follower than a leader, but I was still in the "popular" group all my life. I only had two half-brothers that I rarely saw, so I was influenced at home more by my sisters. However, my close friends often had older brothers, so we'd find out "things" sooner than if we just went through life without them.

This often led to doing "fun" things that we were not supposed to be doing (the normal things, I don't need to expand!). Now I know that many of these things were wrong, or sins, but at that point I really had little to no regret or conviction when I did them. It was fun, naughty, got some laughs, you learned some new things, and life went on. The goal was just not to get caught by your parents, teachers or the police.

We were not actively trying to hurt anyone, but we were self-centered and took risks that put others in harm or made them feel inferior or hurt. Or we just did "fun" things to get a kick out of it. To be honest, I'm glad that there was no such thing as cell phones at that time, as I'm sure we would have gotten in even more trouble.

I was considered one of the friends most likely to take on a dare and do something more risky—I guess that is in my DNA. This usually had to do with driving a car (before we had driver's licenses and sometimes with alcohol in our system), and with motorcycles, mostly offroad, really cool dirt bikes, such as outrunning the cops when they periodically found us.

I was book smart but quite dumb when it came to thinking about how these risky behaviors could hurt or end my life or others. Thank the Lord that I made it through those years without significant injury or even death to me or others.

When I was almost 19, I started dating a young lady that was different than others that I had known or dated. She started telling me about her personal relationship with Jesus Christ and how important it was to her. As we dated for a few months her mom was also very engaging relative to learning about the Bible, and we would have back-and-forth deep discussions on faith, religion and the Bible regularly.

During the first two years of my college I started going to church with them on most of the weekends that I was back in town from college. About two years after meeting this young lady and hearing about the need to have Jesus as a personal savior, not just a "god out there somewhere" relationship, I stopped and bowed my head and asked Jesus to come into my life and to be my Lord and Savior. I put my full trust and faith in the God of the Bible, in Jesus. That day changed my life forever.

After that I slowly started walking in the direction of the light of the Bible. As I continued to go to a Bible-preaching good church and started praying on my own (and with others) and started really reading the Bible for the first time, I found that a lot of my sinful behaviors (not all!) started to melt by the wayside.

One example is my swearing—I essentially immediately stopped swearing. Another one was my drinking; after some time (a year or two), I put a full stop to drinking any alcohol. Now, that hasn't lasted my whole life, but I do try hard to live by "do not get drunk on wine (or any alcohol or drug!)" that the Bible is clear about. But most important, I started really digging into what a deeper relationship with Christ is all about.

One practical tool that I used often in my very early converted years, was the *Our Daily Bread* devotional. It was a printed very small booklet that had a practical reading regarding scripture verses for each day. Those booklets were literally my lifeblood of my early days trusting and trying to follow Jesus. You can still find the digital or printed copy option at www.odbm.org.

Probably the biggest step in this transition was when I changed colleges to the University of Minnesota, Minneapolis campus, and I found a college Bible-based young-adult group called InterVarsity (www.intervarsity.org). I nearly fell over when I went to my first meeting with them.

These cool college students were worshiping the Lord in song and spirit, and it was the most inviting and refreshing thing I had ever witnessed in my life up until that point. I dove into that group and grew some more. Thank you InterVarsity Christian Fellowship!

Eventually I married that young lady after five years of dating and now we've been married for over 30 years and have three adult children. I got my master's degree in civil/structural engineering and became a licensed Professional Engineer. I have worked as a structural engineer designing buildings all of my career and it's one area I feel I give back by providing jobs to many people in the US and abroad. I love my job and I give my best to it every day, but also try my best to not have it sneak into the number one thing in my life before God, as that is a challenge for me.

My family has attended the same wonderful church all my adult life (Emmanuel, headquartered in Spring Lake Park, Minnesota). I followed the Lord's guidance and got re-baptized as an adult, in my early twenties, at this church, with my wife by my side. Shout out to Pastor Nate, an awesome man of God and leader, as well as all the other leaders and volunteers at this church!

APPENDIX -- MY STORY

I've continued living out my faith with the common ups and downs that all Christians have. I am not involved in any leadership within the church but just an average person focusing on faith, family and my job.

Having a personal relationship with Jesus has not made me perfect, by any means, of course, and never will. No one is "perfect" (or sinless) except God/Jesus. Being saved has not made everything in my life go smoothly and I've had to get through a number of things, both self-inflicted and seeming for no reason at all.

I've been through some major challenges and setbacks in my life, personally, at my job and financially. Being saved doesn't mean you have a carefree life with no struggles; however, what it does is give you is one source of immense hope and comfort (Jesus) to walk through these valleys and bruises of life with you.

In my experience, I can say that life as a believer is a continuous struggle to try to orientate yourself towards God and shed the things of the world that clearly aren't what God wants you to do and they have no real value here on Earth or in Heaven. The highlights of this relationship with Jesus is really finding peace and joy with and through Him. Not every day or every moment, but you truly feel the peace, freedom, love and joy from our Father in Heaven, often!

At times you truly feel so much joy that you do actually feel the presence of the Holy Spirit in your life—a real feeling from God, not something you are imagining. That's the gist of what I've experienced with my walk with Christ. Always striving to get closer to Jesus and trying hard to rely on Him (not our own strength) in each and every opportunity and challenge of life.

The thought process and early work for this book started 23 years ago, believe it or not (I'm slow!). God put it in my heart to write this book by a nudging (a feeling) from the Holy Spirit that it was part of my calling. I started categorizing the scripture from the Gospels during my daily bus commutes to and from work, and some flights to jobsites for my job.

After creating the outline and the meat of the scriptures in the main groupings (Chapter 3: Sections 3.1-3.5, in this book) in the early 2000s I briefly picked it back up in 2011 to start the first digital rough draft. Again, my job gave me some long commute time to do this, on trips to South East Asia to run a new office in the Philippines.

Then, in the summer of 2023, I gave it new life by starting to pull it together in a real focused way, since I had an extended professional sabbatical break (thanks to the new company policy!). My goal is simply to follow the will of the Lord and bring this to completion after so many years. This is not a brainchild of my own and I'm not trying to hit anyone over the head with the fear of Hell. I'm just driven to be obedient to the Lord and finally complete and share this book to others to find the true joy, peace and love of Christ.

The approach to this book follows my personality and DNA. As a structural engineer, I design buildings and other large structures. Our methodologies are all founded on analytical science and physical testing. The results are essentially black and white for nearly

APPENDIX -- MY STORY

all principles and processes. There is one right answer when it comes to proving if the physics of the situation works (called statics for building design).

In a similar way, my heart led me to write this book knowing that the Gospel is also very black and white—it has very clear and hard lines between what is true and what isn't. Even though these black and white lines of the Bible cause disagreement, anger, and even worse in the world, it is what it is. As the saying goes, we can talk about anything in a mixed crowd except politics and religion, right?

The Bible has survived history because of testing. The Gospel is similar to physics—it points to one true answer, and that answer is Jesus Christ. The answer is that there is only one way to go to Heaven and be with the one true God of the universe, and that is through true faith in Jesus Christ.

The gift of Heaven and conversion to followers of Christ is not earned by us at all—it's simply a wonderful, loving gift from God. So, this book is a reflection of the science I grew up with and it is organized in a manner that shows the proof of the words of Jesus himself. They are black and white, not gray! There is only one way.

As you can see, my life has not been remarkable or really special, just average or relatively normal/benign. The most important day in my life was when God allowed me to truly trust in Him and ask Him to be my savior. Things have not been perfect from that point on, but God has been very faithful.

God says that He will "never leave us or forsake us,"

and I know that is true from my 30+ years trying to follow Him. My greatest joy in my life comes from the Lord—I do feel His love and His closeness through the Holy Spirit on a regular basis.

I'm not the best at witnessing one-on-one; it's something I need to keep working on. However, God has made it clear that I need to write, finish and distribute this book, and that is part of my calling.

My hope and prayer is that each person reading this book is drawn to really give Jesus a try. That each of you will stop and really ponder this situation. That each of you will, at a minimum, read the New Testament book of Matthew (or any of the Gospels) and the Book of Acts. It doesn't take long, I promise! What do you have to lose?

This is really a life-or-death decision and there is so much upside to securing your place in Heaven. I want all of you to find that!

If for any reason you would like to contact me, you can reach me at Jerodhoffman11@gmail.com or www.jerodhoffman.com.

Blessings to you!

Jerod